I Am A Masterpiece

Tammy Mayer

First edition published by Legacy Therapy, LLC
dba Legacy Therapy Publishing.

Publisher: Laura Mitchell, Legacy Therapy, LLC Denver, CO 80227
Contact: www.legacytherapypublishing.com   www.iamlauramitchell.com

Editor: Donna Davenport Hilliard

Photo Credit: Colleen Perez

Warning – Disclaimer

The purpose of this book is to educate and entertain. The author and/or publisher do not guarantee that anyone following these techniques, suggestions, tips, ideas, or strategies will become successful. The author and/or publisher shall have neither liability nor responsibility to anyone with respect to any loss or damage caused, or alleged to be caused, directly or indirectly by the information contained in this book

The following excerpts were reference with credit to the original author and publisher:

DaVinci Reference: Hilary Weaver and published by vanityfair.com
Michael Angelo Reference: Ben Cerullo and published by Inspiration Ministries, titled "God's Masterpiece"

Dedications

This book is dedicated to:

To my son's Chuck and David, because of your love; I had the perseverance and courage through the hardest times of our lives. No matter the circumstance, we have always loved and strengthened each other. I am blessed beyond measure of the men of God you have both grown to become!
~ Love you ~ Mom

To my beautiful grandchildren and great-grandchildren,
I share with you my story and tell each of you, "You are a beautiful masterpiece!" ~ Nana

To my beautiful Mother, Isabelle Pacheco,
You have always been my rock. You have been my mother, my friend, my counselor, and my prayer warrior.
~ I love you, mama ~ Tammy

Testimonials

Minister Tammy has overcome some of the hardest situations a woman can find herself in. As a survivor of abuse and rejection, she has been able to rise up from the ashes of her circumstances and become a true beauty of God's masterpiece. Her passion for seeing women healed, restored, and empowered is very evident in her ministry. Tammy is a powerful prayer warrior, has a servant's heart, and walks in true humility. I believe that after reading this book, many women will be healed restored and find hope once more.

Tammy, as your pastors, we are very proud of you and can't wait to see the fullness of God's purpose fulfilled in your life and ministry. We love you.

Pastor Veronica and Randy Lucero
Senior Pastors, Word Alive Ministries
Thornton, Colorado

Minister/Evangelist Tammy Mayer is a prophetic voice to the present generation. She has a breaker anointing, bringing deliverance, revelation, and empowerment to a NOW generation. Minister/Evangelist Tammy Mayer has been a staff member of Faith International Ministries in Sanger, California, and has served on our Pastoral team in 2001-2003. She effectively administered the gifts of the Holy Spirit. Minister/Evangelist Tammy Mayer will continue to bless many lives and inspiring and raising up others to operate in the power of the Holy Spirit. We believe this book will shine a light on the power of God's love to heal and restore the broken-hearted.

Apostle Andrew Barraza & Pastor Ami V. Barraza
Faith2Faith Christian Fellowship
Sanger, California

Testimonials

To those seeking a breakthrough and deliverance from physical illnesses or spiritual attacks, chains, hindrances, or just simply failures in life, Tammy is a living instrument of the power of God at work.   Practical, personal, and absolutely relevant in today's world of spiritual blindness and failure. Tammy's ministry of heart healing strikes at the very center of blockages to be removed. She is a minister with the gift of healing, through God's message; she lights the way of healing of the heart first, to open the doors to physical healing and a changed life and on to an active relationship with God, full of fruit, hope, and results.

Dallas Richardson
EDI Consultant
Big Sandy, Tennessee

Have you ever felt the presence of the Lord? The anointing of the Holy Spirit? Minister Tammy Mayer has experienced and shared such things with such power and prayer. She is gifted in the areas of ministering the word of God, prophecy, discernment, healing, and word of knowledge. The Lord has used Tammy in a way that his presence has been brought forward with a sweet, calming, healing atmosphere. Minister Tammy has a heart for the broken, and I know this book "I Am A Masterpiece" will impact your life greatly with healing and hope!

Judy Martinez
Technical Teacher
Thornton, Colorado

Testimonials

Tammy Mayer is one of the most spiritual women I know, her love for Christ is very evident what she does and says is truly shining through her. She is a beautiful and strong leader and a blessing to many. I am very proud of her in this new venture that God has opened up for her. God bless you, my dear friend

Elaine Romero
Minister and Author of the Book, PERSERVERE
Denver, Colorado

Acknowledgments

I acknowledge that without the help of the Holy Spirit, I would not have been able to write this book. As I began to write, it was the Lord who gave me the words to put in this book. I am nothing without my Lord Jesus Christ!

I acknowledge the wonderfully gifted ministers that have imparted into my life over the forty-three years that I have known the Lord Jesus Christ. There are so many of you who have loved and supported me over the years.

I acknowledge Chaeli Annalise, my beautiful granddaughter, for being my model on my book cover. Thank you.

I acknowledge divine appointments, and one of those appointments brought me to my Publisher, Laura Mitchell. Thank you, Laura, for this amazing opportunity that you provided for me to write my story. I am forever grateful!

I acknowledge Donna Davenport Hilliard for the hours she spent editing my book. I am thankful for you!

I acknowledge my beautiful family and friends who have supported and prayed me through as I wrote this book. I love you all!

Note from the Author

In this book, I have shared from my heart about how I felt going through the specific time frames of my life. Other people involved in my life may view the specific details a little differently than I have shared in these pages, I am telling the stories as I saw them unfold and lived them.

I also express the pain, trauma, and the fear I endured, as I reveal pieces of my life that attributed to the wounds I lived for many years, and how I was set free by God's love and his inner healing of my soul. This book reveals how to heal your inner hearts from wounds from the past and the present.

God sees me as a beautiful masterpiece created with his hands, as he sees all who call him Father.

You don't have to live the life of a victim but live a life of victory! Finding joy in life again and knowing that you are loved beyond measure by the one who calls you his masterpiece! With one touch of God's love, he can restore you to the fullest, and you can be the person he created you to be!

Table of Contents

Chapter 1

I Am A Masterpiece

Ephesians 2:10 - New Living Translation
"We are His masterpiece, created in Christ Jesus for good works, which God prepared beforehand that we should walk in them."

We are His Masterpiece, a work of outstanding artistry. Each of us is a work of art carefully designed to be one of a kind created with perfection. If you were to meet me today; you would see a confident, strong woman full of joy and love. It has been a long journey, and it has taken many years to get to this place of peace and joy in my life.

We all have a story to tell. My story is about love, abandonment, abuse, and brokenness and how one touch from God restored, healed the wounds, and gave me the strength to reclaim my heart again. He taught me about the inner healing of my soul and delivered me out of the pain I carried for so many years. I am no longer a victim, but I have arisen from the ashes with beauty and strength.

Strength came and still comes from walking daily with my Lord. I have come to know him as my Abba Father, and I know how he sees me. In 2004 I was ordained as a Minister, and I have a calling for the wounded and hurting hearts. The Lord led me on my journey of inner healing, and now I teach and guide others through the process of inner healing and freedom.

As a young girl of sixteen, I had a beautiful encounter with Jesus at an altar in a small Assembly of God church. My mother had been invited to this little church. She brought me and my sister, Ami, with her. This church service was so different, and nothing like the church we previously attended. The congregation began to sing and clap their hands in praise. I was so surprised when the group started to sing songs of worship. I sensed a change in the atmosphere. Tears began to run down my cheeks as I sang these songs with all my heart. I felt a warmth cover me, and I knew this was the presence of God. I raised my hands and voice and worshiped with all my being. The praise and worship I experienced that evening was no comparison to the quiet hymns in our prior church

My parents had taken my siblings and myself to church every Sunday, and my mother taught us to pray, but I was always searching for more, and I had found it.

That evening when the minister gave an invitation to come to the altar, I knew I wanted to give my life to Jesus. I wept until I had no more tears because of this love that poured over me. I had never experienced a love like this. I didn't want to move. It felt like a warm blanket had been placed around me. There was a sense of feeling safe and loved.

This was the beginning of my life journey of knowing Jesus as the lover of my soul, and I was so desperate to know him even more; there was such hunger that stirred within me. The desire to know Jesus more and more has never stopped. It has only grown

stronger.

In my younger days, I made decisions that lead to two broken marriages which I endured trauma, mental abuse, physical abuse, and abandonment. I was a broken, beaten woman, and I became a person that I did not recognize. I lost myself along the way and desperately longed to find me again. Out of my brokenness, the Lord gave me beauty for ashes and believe me at one time in my life; I was so broken and had almost become a pile of dust. I didn't know how Jesus would put me back together again, and it's true nothing is impossible for the one who first loved us and created us as his very own masterpiece.

Through the journey of my life, I have grown to understand the meaning of being a masterpiece and knowing the one who created me and how God so loves me.

Ephesians 1:4 - The Passion Translation (TPT)
"And he chose us to be his very own, joining us to himself even before he laid the foundation of the universe! Because of his great love, he ordained us, so that we could be seen as holy in his eyes with an unstained innocence."

I see myself so imperfect with so many flaws, but the Father will always see me through the eyes of love as a beautiful masterpiece he took time to create. It takes my breath away to know there is someone that feels this way about me! The Father loves what he has created, and I hear him say, "Look in my mirror Tammy and see what I see, my beautiful creation, my treasure, my beautiful masterpiece." "I created you as a priceless princess with a purpose, I created you in my image, and you are a piece of the Master."

His Workmanship

We call his workmanship—Poiema the original Greek word meaning poem or a work of art. The word of God says I was first a thought. The Father created you and me to share his love with us. He loves us simply because we are his children; he desired each one of us and held each of us in his heart before we were formed in our mother's womb.

Jeremiah 1:5 – The Message (MSG)
"Before I shaped you in the womb, I knew all about you. Before you saw the light of day, I had holy plans for you."

From my beginning, Father God desired more than anything to pour his love into me. He took his time and weaved every little detail of my being. You see, when God created me, with every stroke of his brush, he poured his love onto me a blank canvas. I was uniquely created. Every stroke of my features was delicately constructed to perfection and

I was fearfully and wonderfully made with love. You see, he created every detail of the perfect smile that would light up my face. I may have traits of my parents; however, I am one of a kind I am not a copy. No other person has my laugh or my fingerprints. I am unique. I am a masterpiece, a work of art, a beautiful poem written with great love.

I think of the great painters of our time Da Vinci, Monet, Picasso just to name a few, and how long each of their paintings took to create. Such detail in every stroke on a plain canvas that

was brought to life with the beauty of color.

Psalm 139:13-14 - The Passion Translation (TPT)
"You formed my innermost being, shaping my delicate inside and intricate outside, and wove them all together in my mother's womb."

I thank you, God, for making me mysteriously complex!

Everything you do is so marvelously breathtaking. It simply

amazes me to think about it! How thoroughly, you know me, Lord!

I Am Treasured

Have you ever felt treasured? In the book of Exodus 19:5, it speaks of us being a treasure to the Father. A prized possession.

The Father handpicked us; he chose you and me, and we are of exceptional value to him. You are God's masterpiece. I once read an article written by Ben Cerullo and published by Inspiration Ministries titled "God's Masterpiece" and it read like this, " Like a beautiful poem, He has put considerable thought into the rhyme and rhythm of each of our lives. Think about that for a moment as God's work of art, he put more thought into your creation than Michelangelo put into his paintings on the ceiling of the Sistine Chapel. The Creator spent more time crafting you than Robert Frost did on all his poems combined."

God creates with such beauty look at the constellations or the beautiful galaxies he created with such splendor.

He paints a sunrise and a sunset every evening with brilliant colors. How much more does he pour into creating his children? When I look at the painting called Irises in Monet's Garden by Claude Monet, I see such beauty on the canvas of that painting. The beautiful colors are so vibrant, and there is so much detail that makes the painting come alive.

A masterpiece is not created overnight; a painter or a sculptor puts a lot of time and effort into making a piece of art. As God's masterpiece, he took time with every detail until he had perfected you and me. A painter develops a lot of pride for his painting and pours his heart into this canvas and watches as it comes to life with each stroke of his brush.

Once completed, many present their artwork in public places or galleries. God put a lot of time and thought into creating each of his children. God says even before he made the world, he knew us and loved us.

A Priceless Work of Art

We are God's priceless work of art. Do you ever see yourself as priceless? We are each a priceless work of art to the Father. He created us each to be unique in every way. When the Father looks at you and me, he sees beauty and greatness.

Let's look at an article written by Hilary Weaver in VanityFair.com. She reported, "Leonardo da Vinci's painting "Salvator Mundi" is the most expensive work of art ever sold. In 2017 it sold for $450 million and was considered a priceless work of art. "

How about the Mona Lisa, the world's most famous painting by Leonardo Da Vinci. It took several years to complete the picture. However, when God looks at us, he sees each one of his children as a priceless work of art!

He created each one of us as a priceless work of art full of divine potential. He created you and me to do things that no one else could do in this entire world.

There are many copies of the famous paintings; however, a copy does not have as much value as an original. You are not a copy of someone else; you are unique to you, and I am a treasure to the Father.

The Bible confirms the Father's thoughts.

Psalm 139:18 – English Standard Version (ESV)

"If I would count them, they are more than the sand. I awake, and I am still with you."

Why does the Father love us so much? The same reason the artist loves his paintings. We all matter to the Father! God's greatest masterpiece of creation is you, and it's me. We are a masterpiece, a portrayal of pure love, for you are put together by the Creator up above.

When an artist paints, he paints variations of shadows and lights to reflect the image he is painting on the canvas.

The Father fashioned us into his likeness, using both darkness and light to highlight his work within us so that we can reflect his image to the world,

You are God's work of art, HIS poem, HIS masterpiece!

Isaiah 49:16 – New International Version (NIV)
"See I have engraved you in the palms of my hands."

Chapter 2

My Canvas is Torn and Tattered

When you look at the canvas of your life, what do you see? Are there straight lines, or is your canvas stained from the things that you have gone through in life? Is your canvas stained by the choices you've made?

You may say to yourself, "Me? A masterpiece? I don't think so! Look at the messy lines and torn edges that I created with the choices I have made in life."

What would you give to start all over again? How much money would you pay to have your messy, torn-up canvas turned into a masterpiece? How can I fix my canvas to become a beautiful masterpiece again? Look at my life; how can I ever be called a masterpiece? When I look in the mirror, I don't see a masterpiece I see a total mess!

The enemy knows our weakness and studies each of us at every opportunity. The word of God tells us the enemy comes to steal, kill, and destroy. He tricks us into thinking we are not good enough, and we walk through life broken and defeated.

This enemy is crafty. He tries to rob us of our true destiny by the lies he tells us, and there are times we begin to believe the lies about ourselves. "No one is going to want you! Look at yourself; you're fat, you're ugly, you're not smart enough." The enemy knows how to make us feel worthless if we listen to him.

The last thing the enemy wants to see is you moving forward in your life and seeing yourself as God sees you. This enemy wants you to stay dormant. The enemy wants you to stay stuck in this place of defeat. It's easier to remember to look back at your past and carry it with you than to pay attention to where God wants to take you.

There have been times in my life when I was so broken and defeated. I felt buried beneath a weight of guilt and shame. I lost myself along the way, and I didn't know how to get back to me. I believed the lies of the enemy. I had no self-worth because of the pain and trauma in my life.

There are many wounds in my soul from regret, unmet expectations, betrayal, abandonment, physical and verbal abuse. Because of the verbal abuse about my weight, I had an eating disorder, and I abused my body. I was a broken and defeated woman.

The word of God declares each of us is a masterpiece that he created. When I look back on my life, I wonder how God ever saw me as a masterpiece. Maybe at the beginning of my life, my canvas looked like a beautiful masterpiece, but as I walked through life, my once beautiful canvas was stained, dirty, and ripped in so many places. How could God still see me as his Masterpiece?

My Story

I found Jesus at the age of sixteen and loved being in church. I joined the choir and loved going to the youth group. I was learning how to have a relationship with Jesus, and I knew my life would never be the same. I was so in love with Jesus! I had a hunger to know him deeper, and he was the focus of my life until I met a green-eyed young man that stole my heart and changed my destiny.

I was going into my senior year of high school and excited that I was going to graduate. I was planning my future. I was going to make the most of my last year. I grew up in a small town named Alamosa, Colorado. Most of the senior class, which was around fifty students, had been my friends since kindergarten.

My life changed in November of 1977 when I met a young man who made me laugh and was such a charmer. It didn't hurt that he was handsome and had the most beautiful green eyes and auburn hair.

A friend named Eve had taken me under her wing at church. We spent a lot of time together. She was a year older than me, and I looked up to her in so many ways. Eve's new boyfriend Tony was coming to visit from Denver, Colorado, which was two hours away, and he was bringing his friend Billy with him. Eve wanted Billy and me to meet.

I went to Eve's house that Saturday afternoon, she was so excited to see her boyfriend. When Tony and his friend, Billy pulled up to her house, I peeked through the front window. I was so curious to see this friend. When the passenger door opened, and Billy stepped out the door, my heart began to beat fast. He was so handsome with his auburn hair, green eyes, and beautiful smile. I couldn't wait to meet him!

When Tony and Billy came into the house, I could feel I had butterflies in my stomach, and it felt like my heart was pounding inside my chest. The moment Billy walked in, our eyes met, and we couldn't help but smile at each other. Eve introduced me to Tony, and Tony introduced us both to his friend. Billy looked at me, he smiled and said, "Wow, it's so nice to meet you!" He must have felt the way I did because he suddenly looked nervous. Billy and I had an instant connection.

Billy was charming, and he had a great sense of humor. We sat and talked for the next hour, getting to know each other. I felt like a magnet was pulling us together. That evening, the four of us went to dinner, and by the time we headed back to Eve's house, I felt like I had known Billy all my life.

I was so comfortable around Billy because he was easy to talk to, and we had so much in common. As I got ready to leave, and Billy asked me if I would like to have lunch with him after church on Sunday. Billy wanted to spend more time with me before he had to go back home. I told him I would love to but had to check with my parents and would let him know after church.

That evening as I lay on my bed, I played over the moments I spent with Billy that day. I know I had just met him, but I liked him and wanted to get to know him better. I had such a good time with him. I never laughed like the way I did with him. I couldn't wait to see him again!

The next day after church, I joined Billy, Tony, and Eve for lunch. I had butterflies in my stomach when I saw him walking toward me. Billy had a big smile, and when I saw him, I felt weak, my legs felt like jelly, and I thought, "What is going on with me? I feel so lightheaded." I took a deep breath as he walked toward me, and I couldn't stop smiling. I had never felt like this before.

Billy asked me for my phone number and address. He promised to write letters. In 1977 we did not have cell phones. The only phone that was in my home was in the kitchen. There was no texting, only letter writing.

I was so excited because this handsome young man liked me and wanted to get to know me. Although I knew we lived two hours from each other, I thought to myself, "We can be friends and get to know each other."

As they were leaving, Billy hugged me and said, "I really like you, and I promise I will write to you. I promise to come and see you again."

I smiled and replied, "I like you, too, and look forward to seeing you again." He looked in my eyes and said, "I wish I didn't live so far. I would be spending every day with you. You are so beautiful!"

My stomach was doing flips, and my heart was beating so fast I thought it was going to fall out of my chest! He gave me another big hug and kissed my cheek, and he looked into my eyes and said, "I'm not saying goodbye, I know I will see you again. I'll see you soon, pretty girl."

My heart skipped a beat to hear Billy say I was beautiful and that he liked me as much as I liked him. It wasn't going to be easy just writing letters, but I was going to see how this turned out. I wondered if he was going to keep in touch with me. I thought about him all night, and it was hard to fall asleep. I knew I had to get up early for school the next day. I prayed, "Lord, thank you for my new friend, Billy. Keep him safe. I don't want him to be a distraction. Please help me to keep my eyes on you."

I received my first letter from Billy on Friday. I didn't expect to hear from him, but this was the beginning of our relationship. We wrote back and forth for the next month, getting to know about each other and our families. I would get so excited when I would get home from school, and there was a letter waiting for me. I would run up to my room and read it over and over again. I had to keep my heart guarded. I did not want to get hurt by this guy. He was handsome, and I knew there had to be other girls he may have been interested in back in Denver where he lived.

After six weeks of letters, he wrote and told me he would be coming back to visit the next weekend with Tony. I called Eve, and she confirmed Tony and Billy would be visiting. It would be nice to see Billy again. I had an excitement deep in my heart, and I counted the days until I could speak to him face to face.

Friday evening rolled around, and I got a call, It was Billy. He wanted me to know he was in town and was staying with Tony and his family. He was happy and told me he wanted to see me that evening, but Tony had made plans to hang out with his uncle. I was disappointed that I wouldn't be seeing Billy that night, but I didn't want him to know. I told him that I looked forward to seeing him the next day.

The following day, I was waiting for him at Eve's house, and when he walked through the door, he was grinning from ear to ear. He was so handsome. His green eyes sparkled, and he gave me a big hug and said, "I missed you so much, thank you for writing to me. I checked the mailbox every day, and I looked forward to receiving each letter from you!" We spent as much time as we could while he was in town and I was sad when he left.

We had so much fun. Billy always made me laugh with his crazy jokes, and he treated me like I was so special to him, and when I looked into those green eyes, I felt like I would melt.

Billy faithfully wrote letters to me every week, and sometimes I received one or two letters. I was crazy about him and couldn't wait to see him again. Several weeks passed, and we continued to write letters and talk on the phone. Billy was saving money to buy a car. He didn't want to wait for his friend to make a trip to see me.

One day Billy called with good news. He purchased a car and was planning to come to visit that weekend. He said, "I really miss you and have to see you!"

I was so excited when he got to town early Saturday morning, and we spent the day together. He bought me a record, and the song was named "Always and Forever." He said, "I want to be with you forever!" My heart was beating so quickly that I thought it was going to jump out of my chest; this happened each time I was around Billy. I was in love with this young man, and I knew I wanted to be with him always and forever.

A Promise

On my eighteenth birthday, Billy gave me a promise ring and said, "One day, I will marry you." I was so in love with Billy. My heart ached every time he traveled back home. I couldn't wait for the day we could be together. We continued our long-distance relationship through the end of our senior year in high school.

I graduated from high school in May of 1978. I talked to my parents about moving to Denver and staying with my aunt. My mother contacted my aunt, and she agreed. My parents bought me a car to make sure I traveled to Denver safely.

I got a job at the mall and spent my free time with Billy. He played fastpitch softball. He was a pitcher, and we were at the ballpark most of the time. We were inseparable. We grew closer and began talking about our future and getting married. Little did I know marriage would come sooner than I had planned.

When I moved to Denver, I intended to find a home church, I never did. My focus was on Billy and spending time with him. I fell away from God. My heart's desire was no longer him, but Billy.

In November, I discovered I was pregnant. I was so scared and confused. I was only eighteen and thought, "How could I be a mom"? I didn't know what to do. I called my sister but didn't know my dad was listening on the other end of the phone line. My dad was so hurt. I broke his heart.

My dad called me a few days later and said, "You don't have to get married. Your mother and I will help you raise the baby, and you can go to college." I told my dad Billy asked me to marry him, and I loved him. I wanted to get married. My father told me he loved me and would always be there for me, and if this were the choice, he would help me.

Billy and I decided to get married in February. I was so excited to plan the wedding. We had a small wedding in Denver, and we moved in with my new mother-in-law and her husband. As a new young bride, I had hopes of being happy with the handsome man I married.

Looking back, we were so young, thinking that love would be enough. At the time, I could not have imagined the heartache I would endure being Billy's wife!

Married and So Alone

I had grown up in a small town, sheltered, and had not experienced much in life. Now I was a wife and soon to be a mother. I was scared about being both. I didn't know how to be a wife. I was a young girl with fantasies of how marriage should be. There were times I would hear women that had been married for ten or fifteen years say they had been so lonely in their marriage. I could never understand that comment until I experienced it myself. I thought when Billy and I were married; we would be able to spend so much time together. For the first few months, I was in bliss. We were inseparable, and I got to know his family and friends. I was so happy until things began to change, and Billy started to take me for granted.

After the excitement of being married had worn off, I found myself alone most of the time. Billy had a job painting cars. Every evening after he ate dinner, he was off to the youth center to play basketball with his friends.

I spent little time with Billy. I cried a lot, and I was so lonely. My body was changing, as my belly grew. I was miserable. I reminisced about being anxious to graduate and excited about moving away to start a life with Billy. I thought my life with him was going to be wonderful. The life I was living was not the life I imagined, and there were many times I regretted taking the path that I did.

After Billy left to play basketball, I would walk to a grade school playground on the hill near our home, where I would sit on a swing and cry. I didn't feel love or affection from my husband. I remember thinking, "Marriage is not supposed to be like this."

I would sit and talk to God, but I felt like I had failed him. I was so on fire for the Lord until I met Billy, then he became my God. I was such a foolish young girl with dreams and false expectations. I wept and asked God to forgive me for thinking of myself and putting him on a shelf. I was so ashamed of the decisions I had made and repented of everything I had done.

I heard God tell me, "I still love you! I will never leave you or forsake you." I felt the warmth of his embrace, and a feeling of peace came over me.

I couldn't stop the tears from falling as I sat on that swing. I knew I had placed myself in this predicament, and the thought depressed me. The only thing I knew to do was to pray and ask God to change the situation. I hated feeling so alone and empty.

I looked at my situation and realized I didn't know Billy when I married him. If I would have known I would be alone, I would never have said, "I do!" I would have stayed with my family and raised my baby with their guidance.

I was his wife, and I needed him to be a husband. Each time I would tell Billy how I felt and ask him to spend more time with me, he would say, "I work all day and need to get away and play ball with my friends. Besides, I am only away for a couple of hours!"

Billy was constantly saying he didn't realize he married a nag. When all I was trying to do was communicate. I would tell him, "by the time you get home, you're tired and want to go to sleep. You don't spend time with me. Almost every weekend, you make plans to meet up with your friends and leave me behind. We are never together! Don't you love me? " I asked. "Because when you love someone, you want to spend time with them!".

He replied, "I do love you, but I like to play ball, and you can't take that away from me." Every evening was the same, he would eat dinner, we would end up fighting, and off he would go to the youth center, and I would get angry and frustrated.

Each time my mom would call, I would tell her I was happy and doing fine. I couldn't share my heart with her. I held on to my hurt and buried it. She would ask if my belly was growing and how I was feeling. My mom was so excited about being a grandma, and she would tell me she missed me so much.

Every time I spoke with my mom, I wanted to go back home. I regretted ever meeting Billy. I would talk to the Lord and pray, "Please help me, Lord. I don't want to be in this situation. Please give me strength. I can't make it here without you!" Sorrow filled the depth of my heart. I was alone in this so-called marriage. I loved Billy, but I hated how he treated me.

Rescued

When I was eight months into my pregnancy, my mother drove to Denver to visit me. She took one look at me and knew something was wrong. I was so swollen, and she saw the sadness in my eyes. She said to me, "I am taking you home to take care of you!"

She was so angry, she yelled at Billy. "You haven't taken care of her! She doesn't look good, I am afraid for her, and I am taking her back home to Alamosa with me!"

Billy didn't argue with my mom. He helped me pack my things and told me, "I'm sorry I haven't been the best husband, and I haven't taken care of you. I have been selfish, and I haven't been around much. It's best if you go with your mom. She will take better care of you, and I know you will probably be happier. I promise I will call you and see you as soon as I can."

Billy looked sad, and I saw remorse in his eyes. Maybe he did love me but didn't know how to show it. I was ready to leave. I was worn. I didn't know if I wanted to be married anymore. I knew for sure I did not want to come back to the same life, especially with a baby!

I was happy to be leaving. Although my heart was heavy and broken because of the way things had turned out between Billy and me, this wasn't the marriage that I had envisioned. Perhaps time away from each other would change things between us.

I was not well. I was so big, and every part of me swollen, my feet were so big, and my shoes did not fit. I did go to my regular doctor appointment visits, and the doctor always said I was doing good. I was looking forward to having my mom take care of me. I missed my family so much. My prayers were answered, and I was grateful. I was getting out of the situation I was in, and I didn't know if I would return.

There is a saying that states, "absence makes the heart grow fonder"? I prayed my husband would miss me and would have a change of heart. In all reality, he was a boy trying to be a man. Billy didn't know what marriage was about; neither did I.

I was thankful my wonderful mother had come to see me and took me back with her. She asked me, "Why didn't you let me know how bad things were for you here?"

I answered while crying, "I wanted to work this marriage out, mom, but I realized how you couldn't work on something by yourself, and I didn't want you and dad to worry about me." "You both are so young. I wish you hadn't married. Your dad and I would have helped you with the baby, but I know you were crazy about each other, and you wanted to be with him. I want to see you happy, and you are far from being happy. Maybe this time apart will be good for both of you."

When I got back to our small town of Alamosa, Colorado, and my mother made an appointment with our family doctor, and he diagnosed me with preeclampsia. My blood pressure was high, and every part of my body swollen. I had to rest and keep my feet elevated. I couldn't wear shoes, and my feet hurt so bad. I was scared to have this baby. I didn't know what to expect. My mother was very supportive and would pray with me and tell me, "Trust in the Lord, he will take care of you, and the little one that's coming to bless our home."

I missed Billy. He called me every night to check on me. He worried when I told him about my diagnosis. Billy would tell me how sorry he was and that he loved and missed me so much! He knew what big jerk he had been and how selfish his actions were.

I was happy to be back with my family. It was nice to visit my home church and see my friends. My mom and my sister had a baby shower for me. I received so many wonderful baby gifts. The reality of my baby being here soon had finally hit me. I was getting excited. I already loved this baby so much. I prayed I would be a good mom. I was nineteen and had no idea how my life was going to change.

Before I met Billy, I planned to attend college and maybe travel. I wanted to do so many things. When we are young, we don't realize the choices we make for our lives are like throwing a pebble into a lake and seeing the ripples expand.

My time was getting closer, and Billy was planning to come and see me. He said he missed me and needed to see me. Billy wanted to try and make things right between us. Billy knew his selfishness had caused me to be sick, and he regretted the way he had treated me. I was happy when he pulled up in his car. He gave me a big hug and a kiss. He said, "I missed you so much I couldn't wait to see you."

He showered me with love and affection. I couldn't believe this was the same person I had left a month ago. That evening when we went to bed, I wasn't feeling very well, and In the middle of the night, my water broke. I woke Billy up and told him my water broke, and I was in labor. This baby was in a hurry to come and was going to be two weeks early. He jumped out of bed and was so scared and excited he put his pants on backward. I laughed so hard and told him it's going to take time for this little guy to come, he didn't have to rush!

I woke my parents up, and we all headed to the hospital, twelve miles away. I had natural childbirth. It took twenty-two hours to deliver the baby. With every contraction, I wished I could get out of my body and run; it was so painful.

I delivered a beautiful baby boy, and we named him Charles but decided to call him Chuckie. He had red hair like his daddy and deep dimples. It was love at first sight. I thanked God for being with me through the long delivery and blessing me with a beautiful son. Billy was so happy to see and hold his son. He was in love with this little guy. We knew our lives would never be the same.

Billy stayed a week but had to get back to work. He was sad to leave us. I wasn't going back to the same situation, and I made that clear to Billy. I didn't want to leave until after my six-week follow-up appointment. I needed time to decide if I was going back with Billy or staying with my parents.

Billy and my mother-in-law came to visit us two weeks later. Billy was begging me to go home with him and promised things would be different. He was saving money to get an apartment. He wanted the chance to prove he could be a better husband to me, and a good dad to Chuckie.

I had to pray about returning to Billy because I didn't want to go back to the same situation, especially with a newborn. Billy was so sad when he left and said he would call every day and check on us. Billy promised he would be back in two weeks. I knew he loved Chuckie as much as I did, and I saw the hurt in his eyes when he hugged us both and kissed us goodbye.

My parents never pressured me into staying. They knew I loved Billy, and they did want us to be a family. It was going to be so hard to leave them and go back to Denver. I was so blessed to have such wonderful parents. I knew it was going to be hard on them to have us leave. They had grown attached to Chuckie.

I talked to Billy after my follow-up appointment and told him I would come back with him, but things needed to change. He needed to show me he was going to be a better husband. We had a baby to raise together, and he was going to have to help me with the baby.

Billy was so happy the day he came to get us. We left for Denver the following day. My family had been so supportive. I knew I was going to miss them terribly, and it was hard for my parents to see me and Chuckie leave. They hugged me and told me they were just a phone call away. They would be there for me if I needed to come home again. My father told Billy, "You take care of my girl. I don't want to see her in the condition she came to us; brokenhearted and depressed!" Billy promised both of my parents; he was going to be a good husband and father.

Chapter 3

Broken Promises

After Billy picked us up, we moved in with my mother-in-law. A change had come over him while we were apart; he showed so much love and affection to our son and me. Billy's mom was a big help with Chuckie. She was wonderful, and she enjoyed having her grandson near.

I loved being a mom, but I wished I were home in Alamosa with my family. I missed them and would have liked to be where my mom could help me. Being a new mom was scary. I was grateful I had my mother-in-law helping me with Chuckie. All of the family loved him.

Billy was doing his part, helping with his son, and spent more time with us. He adored his son, and he was becoming a better husband. He would go to work and rush home to spend time with us. I was getting to know my husband again, and I enjoyed being with him. The person I had fallen in love with was back, and I could finally say I was happy again. I forgave him for the way he treated me, and I knew this marriage was going to take work. We both agreed to listen and communicate.

Chuckie was growing fast. I was battling the weight I had gained during pregnancy. It had been nine months, and I still had twenty pounds to shed. I hated being overweight. I felt uncomfortable; my clothes were tight. I was determined to get the rest of the weight off.

Billy started taking a few morning classes at the community college. His boss worked with him so he could do both. And one day he started going to the youth center to play basketball again in the evenings, then it was back to spending less time with his family.

I slowly started to see a change in Billy, he was pulling away again, and nothing I did would satisfy him. He harassed me about my weight. "You are so chubby! What happened to the hot, skinny girl I married?"

I told him, "I'm working on it! I don't like looking the way I do, I had a difficult pregnancy, and it's taking some time!" Billy gave me a disgusted look and walked away. "You're supposed to love me just the way I am!" I yelled. I was furious. There was always something wrong with the way I looked or what I wore. His degrading words hurt me. I just had a feeling in my gut; he was hiding something. He was back to being cold and barely giving attention to Chuckie or me.

"Why don't you stay home tonight to spend time with us? I asked. "I miss you, and never see you much. You promised to be different. You promised if I came back home, we would be important to you, and you wouldn't be selfish!"

He replied, "You're such a nag! I can't stand to be around you. I did promise to be different, but this is who I am. I break promises,"! He gave me a disgusted look and walked away.

I was so miserable again. I wished I had stayed in Alamosa, where I had my family and friends. I felt something was going on with Billy. He wasn't around much, and he treated me cruelly

When Chuckie was nine months old, I knew things needed to change, or I would be returning to my parent's home for good. I didn't sign up to have a husband who was never home and who treated me poorly. I loved and hated him at the same time. I had given my whole heart to this person when I met him at the altar, but I could see things falling apart once again. I began to seek God, asking for direction. I couldn't understand why things between Billy and myself had changed so much. I prayed night after night, "God, please reveal to me what is going on. I can't take this anymore!"

A Knock at the Door

Be careful what you pray for because you just may receive it. The answer may come when you least expect it and turn your life upside down. There was a knock at the door. I answered, and a girl stood there. She said, "Does Billy live here? I'm looking for him. We are supposed to go to prom this weekend, and I wanted to make the final arrangements."

She was dressed in a cheerleader uniform and was a cute girl. My heart dropped. I told her Billy is married, and we have a baby. She didn't care. She said, "I'm Billy's girlfriend, Sara, and we have been dating each other for a while." "Where did you meet Billy"? I asked. "I take classes at the college, and I met him in the cafeteria."

She was so cocky. I wanted to grab her and beat the crap out of her. I took a deep breath. I knew if I beat her up, I would go to jail, and what would happen to my baby? I told her, "Billy is at the youth center across the street. Let's both go talk to him." I figured he couldn't lie about seeing this girl if we were both in the same room with him.

Sara drove her car to the youth center, and I walked. I was so angry. I wanted to kill Billy. I understood why he was so distant and rude to me. He had met a girl, and she was still in high school. I wondered, What the heck was wrong with him?

We walked into the gym, and I told her to go in first, I stayed back. I wanted Billy to see her first. When he saw her, his face lit up, and he had the biggest smile.

I walked into the gym, and as I did his face and grew pale, and he didn't know what to do. I told him, "We need to talk now!" He said, "I don't want to talk to you. Go home. I will talk to you later."

I said, "No, I will not go home. Are you dating this girl? Is this true?" Billy wouldn't look at me or answer me. He kept shooting baskets. I told him, "You better come and talk to me now, or I will make a scene." He was so mad; he grabbed my arm tightly and said, "Go home! I don't want you here!" I pulled my arm away from him and said, "I am not putting up with this! I give you the option right now: do you want your son and me, or do you want her?"

He looked into my eyes and said, "I want her!"

I looked over at Sara, and she had a smug smile on her face. I wanted to grab her by her hair and attack her. Billy saw the look in my eyes and told me to go home and leave her alone!

My heart shattered into a million pieces. I told Billy I was going back to my parents' house, but he didn't care. He walked away and started shooting his basketball again, and I walked out of the youth center.

My heart hurt, and my chest ached, my head was throbbing. I couldn't see through my tears, and I felt as if I could barely breathe. My legs didn't want to move. I wanted to crumble right there on the grass, but I had to get home to the one person who loved me, my son Chuckie.

As I walked back home, I just wanted this sharp, throbbing pain in my heart to stop. I didn't know how I was going to go forward. There was so much rage within me. I was going home to get one of Billy's bats, and I was determined to come back to the youth center and break all the windows out of Sara's car. I would get even with her for wrecking my marriage.

I wanted to beat this girl until there was nothing left of her. How dare she come to my home and take my husband from me. I was going to hurt them both. I started running home. I couldn't wait to come back and get even with Billy and Sara. I couldn't believe this was happening. I kept hearing Billy's voice say, "I want her!" I wanted to punch him in his face and take a bat to both of his legs.

When I walked into the house, I saw my son with his grandma. He was smiling at me with those deep dimples, and I stopped. I thought, "If I take a bat to Sara's car and beat her up, what will happen to my son?"

I had to calm down. I took several breaths. I told myself to breathe, just breathe and calm down. I took my son from his grandma and said to myself, "No one in this world is more important than my beautiful boy!"

Chuckie saved me from making a horrible decision that could have ended my life. I could have ended up in jail, or even prison, with as much rage and anger that I felt. I wanted to take a bat to not only Sara's car but also to Sara. I was planning to wait until she came out of the youth center and attacked her.

I began to say to myself, "Calm down, take a breath, hurting them won't change what he said and did to you!" My head was pounding so hard I thought I was going to pass out. My heart seemed as if it were falling into a million pieces. How could he do this to me? I loved him so much!

I went into my bedroom with my son and kept saying to myself, "Why did he stop loving me?" I looked in the mirror and saw this chubby girl dressed in sweatpants. I began to blame myself, "Look at yourself, you're fat and ugly. Why wouldn't he want someone else?"

My heart was shattered, and the pain was unbearable. I felt like I was going to lose my mind! I picked up my baby and held him close while tears streamed down my face. Somehow holding him gave me a little peace. The smile he gave me calmed me, and I knew I had to give him a better life than the one we were living.

I called my mom and told her what happened. She prayed for me and said, "I'm wiring you money to come home. Your dad and I will help you with the baby. Don't worry. Things will get better. Trust in the Lord. He never fails us in the storms, and he guides us through the storms." My mom has always been a woman of prayer and faith. I felt a peace come over me after talking to her.

My heart felt like it had been stabbed a thousand times and was barely beating. My soul was so wounded. How could I recover from this deception? I didn't know, but I knew to call out to the Lord because he said he would never leave me or forsake me. I cried out, "Please help me, God! It hurts too much!"

I packed up and went to Western Union to pick up the money my mom had sent to me. I couldn't wait to get away from Billy. Maybe the pain in my heart would subside the further I got away from him.

Billy came home later that night and didn't speak to me. He slept on the couch. I got up early the next morning, took my bags, and loaded my car, and said goodbye to my mother-in-law. She was sad to see us go. Before I left, Billy kissed his son and said, "I'm sorry I didn't mean for this to happen."

I looked him in the eye and told him, "Your apology means nothing to me. Do you know how you made me feel in front of that girl? I was so humiliated. You made your choice. I don't want ever to want to see you again. You're dead to me! I hate you! I can't wait to be far away from you!"

As I stared at him, my heart ached. This person promised me the world then crushed my world into a million pieces. I had to be strong. I told him, "Please don't bother me, remember the choice you made! I thought you were the man I would grow old with, but all you have ever done is hurt me with your words and your actions. I didn't deserve what you did to your son and me. I don't want anything to do with you ever again. You don't deserve to see your son. You didn't spend much time being his dad; you were too busy with your little girlfriend to care about him".

Billy looked at me. "Chuckie is still my son, and I want to be able to see him." I shouted at him, "Now that I am leaving, you want to be a dad! You had all the time in the world, but you took him for granted and found someone else to take his place! I don't want to see you!" I took a deep breath, trying to be strong and said goodbye. I was determined to change my life for myself and my son! So many thoughts passed through my mind as I drove home, I kept playing the scene over and over in my head.

Billy had been seeing Sara for some time. That's why he was gone so much, and why he was so mean, moody, and distant with me.

I wondered how many times had he been gone in the evening when he said he was playing basketball and was with her? She knew where to find him. She knew where he lived. Tears started to flow again. The pain in my heart was so intense. I could barely breathe. I felt like Billy had died, and I was mourning him.

I drove for two hours, with tears rolling down my face. I turned the radio on and began to sing. I needed some sort of distraction to stop me from replaying the words said to me, "I want her!" over and over again.

I was devastated; my soul and my spirted was wounded. He had mentally abused me daily with his words because of her. I was so bitter and angry, how was I ever going to heal from this? I started to pray. I prayed for peace.

Broken

Jeremiah 17:14 - The Message (MSG)
"God, pick up the pieces. Put me back together again. You are my praise!"

How would I pick up the pieces of my broken life? I was numb. This time it wasn't only me, I had a beautiful son to take care of. Chuckie needed me, and I needed him.

I still wanted to beat Sara to a pulp and break all the windows of her car. Chuckie saved me from doing the things I wanted to do to Billy and his girlfriend. Chuckie was the most important person in my life. His smile brought me back from depression. My handsome boy with his auburn hair and his beautiful deep dimples was the only guy I wanted in my life! I loved him with everything in my being, and I would do anything to make his life happy.

Within two weeks, I lost the extra weight. I was so numb. I would remember Billy telling me I was fat and giving me a disgusted look. His words hurt and made me feel so ugly. Words are a weapon that pierces the heart and can destroy a person.

Now that I was no longer with Billy, I had to tell myself every time I looked in the mirror, "You are beautiful and not ugly. You are strong. You are a woman of value and worth!" But when I looked in the mirror, I still saw this sad chubby girl staring back at me with her sad eyes. I had to keep saying this out loud until I believed it in my heart.

I would remember the scripture that reads. I am fearfully and wonderfully made, and tell myself, "Every day will get better. Hold on to the hand of God. He said he would never leave you or forsake you." I cried all the time. I would look in the mirror and not recognize the person looking back. I thought, "Who was this broken, beaten person?" I had lost myself along the way. I had been this joyful person with so much life, and now I was felt so broken. It was hard to smile.

It felt like Billy had died, and I was mourning him. I felt empty inside. The rejection was a horrible feeling. I felt like I was not good enough, and my love meant nothing. I felt as if it was the worst time of my life. There were so many unmet expectations with our relationship and marriage. I wished I had never met him. My life had been such a roller coaster with him.

For many months I played the same scene out in my mind. I would beat myself up, wondering why I didn't see the signs, or maybe I did but didn't want to believe something was going on with Billy. I kept hearing the words, "I want her!"

I was so thankful for my wonderful parents that were always there for me and loved me through my pain and helped me to heal slowly. They never judged the situation, and they just stood by my side.

I got a job with the Park Service, and my mom took care of Chuckie. I spent time praying and went to church. I needed God more than anything. Slowly, I began to heal.

The joy of my life was my beautiful son Chuckie. He was growing so fast. He was walking and getting into everything. Every time I looked at my happy little boy, I knew I made the right decision to move home with my family. Chuckie was my parents' first grandson, and they adored him. My son was my joy.

As each month passed, I tried to be strong, but my heart was wounded. I didn't know how it was ever going to mend. Although I had a good job, family, and friends that supported me, I was still battling depression. Every day it was a struggle to get out of bed. I wanted to sleep forever so that the pain would go away.

I liked my job. I was working with a park architect and was encourage to go to college and perhaps pursue a career as an architect. I was now setting goals for my life and putting the past behind me.

Billy hadn't contacted me for over six months. I thought it had been long enough for me not to care anymore, but love doesn't die overnight, especially when you loved that person, and time doesn't heal all wounds. My heart was still very wounded. At times I was only going through the motions.

I couldn't understand why he had not communicated or asked about his son. I decided we were better off without him. Looking back, life with Billy had been so hard. Most of my pregnancy, I was alone; he was always with his friends. I didn't feel loved and appreciated. It wasn't how life was supposed to be.

I felt so alone when I was living with Billy. I thought marriage was going to be different and that Billy would love me and share every part of my life and our son's life, but in reality, I didn't feel loved, just alone!

The Phone Call

Psalm 147:3 – The Passion Translation (TPT)
"He heals the wounds of every shattered heart."

It had been almost seven months when Billy called. My mom answered the phone. "It's Billy. He wants to talk to you. Do you want to take his call?"

I couldn't breathe; my heart was beating so fast, and anger swept over me. I relived the day he didn't want me; the pain in my heart was unbearable. I took a breath and said yes, I would speak to him and took the phone from my mom. "Hello?" I said coldly. I was ready to battle with him! Billy said, "Hi, how are you and Chuckie doing? I'm so sorry for the way I treated you and cheating on you. I miss both of you so much!"

I was so angry! How dare he call me and think everything will be back to normal just by him saying he was sorry! I saw red and told him, "How dare you call me now. We have been gone for months, and out of the blue, you want to say you're sorry! I don't want to speak to you. I hate you, and I hate what you did to both me and Chuckie!" I was fuming. I told him I wasn't ready to speak with him and hung up the phone. I was so angry with him.

Hearing his voice brought all the emotions that I had suppressed back to the surface. Everything I felt on the day when I heard, "I want her!" came flooding back to me again. I was a mess. I went to my room and cried. I was shaking. I had to make myself breathe and calm myself. I cried out to the Lord, "Will this pain ever leave my heart? I can't take this anymore!"

Billy called back a few days later and asked me not to hang up, but to hear him out. I said nothing and let him talk. "I have missed you both so much. My life is not the same without you both! I am so sorry for what I did; I'm sorry for hurting you so badly. I realize I can't live without you and our son. I want you both back in my life again."

I was so angry with him. How dare he call and think that just because he said, "I'm sorry, forgive me," that everything would be forgiven. I told him, "I don't know if I want to go back with you. Chuckie and I are doing just fine without you, and I have moved on with my life." Forgiveness was the furthest from my mind. How could I forgive a person who destroyed me, who crushed me? "Don't think that just because you call, I am going to fall all over you and say yes, we can try again. All these months, you didn't even reach out to find out how your son was doing!"

Billy was quiet for a minute, then he said, "I know, I know, I was so scared to contact you. Do you know how hard it was to call you today? I was shaking. Believe me, I know I put you through so much, and I want to make it up to you. Please give me another chance. Just think about it. Is it ok if I call you again tomorrow?"

I was so angry; I could still hear "I want her" in my mind. Now that he was done playing around, he suddenly wanted his family back. I couldn't even comprehend forgiving Billy. Why would I want to go back to the same situation with him?

I wasn't ready to discuss our relationship and needed time to pray and decide what was best for Chuckie and me. I told him I would call him when I was ready to talk to him again. He understood and agreed to wait until I was ready to speak to him again.

My mom asked if I was alright. I shared my conversation with Billy and told her I was still terribly angry with him and needed time to figure out what was best for Chuckie and me. She told me to pray and ask God to help me forgive and to heal my heart. Mom advised me to ask God for direction. She said, "You know we are all here to support you in whatever decision you make."

How could I just forgive this person who had ripped my heart into a million pieces and made me feel less than nothing? I didn't want to go back to the same life. How did I know he wouldn't do this to me again? I prayed and asked the Lord to heal my heart. I didn't want to carry this pain anymore.

I called Billy the next week and told him I didn't want to go back with him, but he could come and see his son. He thanked me for allowing him to see Chuckie and asked if he could come to Alamosa to visit. I agreed.

I was nervous to see him again. I was still angry, and I wanted to punch him in the face for what he had done. I wasn't going to do that, but he not only had to face me, but he also had to face my family. My dad was not happy. I asked him to be cordial for Chuckie's sake. He agreed.

When Billy pulled up in his car, I thought it best if I met him outside to have some privacy. I picked up Chuckie, and we went out the door. Billy was just getting out of the car when we walked out to the porch.

He looked nervous but put on a big smile and said hi. He looked at Chuckie and couldn't believe how much he had grown and how cute he was. He looked at me and said, "He looks so much like me, can I hold him?" I didn't know if Chuckie would go with him, but he did. Billy was in awe. Tears began to roll down his cheeks as he looked at me and said, "I was such a fool to have lost you and my son. I have missed so much of his life. Do you think you could ever forgive me? I want a chance to make it up to you. I know I hurt you. I was so stupid and selfish."

I looked into Billy's eyes. "I don't know if I can forgive you right now. I know I don't want a life with you, but I will never keep you from your son. as far as you and I being together again, I don't see it happening."

He looked sad, but I wasn't going to give in to him. "Can we at least be friends for Chuckie's sake?" I told him I would try, but I was still very hurt. He stayed the weekend and spent time with Chuckie. When he got ready to leave, he asked if he could come back in two weeks and if he could call and check on Chuckie.

Billy called at least twice a week and came to visit every other weekend. He was desperate to have us back with him. I had to pray for direction. I had to learn to get along with him and not get angry every time I looked at him. I still wanted to punch him in the face every time I was near him, and I told him so.

He said, "If you think it will make you feel better to hit me as hard as you can, I won't stop you. I know I really deserve it!" Of course, I couldn't hit him. I knew if I took a swing at him, I might never stop!

I didn't want to rush back into this marriage. I had trust issues now, which were expected. I did see a change in Billy, and he was trying hard to win me back, but it wasn't going to be that easy.

After months of Billy calling and coming to see us, I eventually gave in and decided to work things out. Chuckie needed both parents to raise him. I moved back to Denver with Billy, but we quickly decided to move to Alamosa where my family lived. I needed to get him away from all his friends and start fresh. Being in the same environment was too hard for me. The memories were always lingering, and I still couldn't trust Billy. I knew it was going to take time until I could fully trust him again.

We moved to Alamosa and lived with my parents until Billy got a job. We were able to move into an apartment. Billy was true to his word, and he became a good husband and a wonderful father. We went to church as a family. I forgave Billy and put everything we had been through in the past and looked forward to a new future. Life was good, and we built a house, and Billy eventually got a job with the City of Alamosa. I got a part-time job at the only pharmacy in town when Chuckie started kindergarten.

After almost six years of marriage, I found out I was going to have a second child. I was excited. Chuckie was happy, and he wanted a baby brother. He told me, "Mommy, I prayed and prayed God would give me a brother, and I know there is a brother in your tummy." He was right. The ultrasound showed I was going to have a son. I was so happy to be adding to our family. Our life seemed settled and going well.

Chapter 4

I Smell Trouble

Billy was acting strange. He was distant, mean, and irritable. I thought to myself, "What is going on with this guy?" The phone would ring late at night, and when I would answer it, I could hear breathing on the other end, and I would just hang up.

While working at the pharmacy, I would hear rumors of Billy cheating on me with other women in town. I would confront him, and he would just laugh and say, "People in this town don't have anything better to do than to make up stories."

I came home one day and couldn't find my keys to the front door. I went around the back door and found him on the phone, laughing. When he saw me, his face grew pale. He hung up quickly and opened the door. I asked him, "Who were you talking to?" He said, "Jerry from work."

I asked him, "Why didn't you open the door for me when you saw me struggling with the bags of groceries?" Billy laughed. "I had to finish my conversation." I knew he was lying; it wasn't just the hormones of being pregnant. "You always read too much into things. Just let it go."

As my pregnancy progressed, I saw the old Billy again. He was distant and cold with me. He stopped going to church with us. His demeanor changed; he was irritable and snappy all the time with me. I prayed that the Lord wouldn't let this be happening again. I couldn't go through the crushing pain again.

When I was six months pregnant, he told me, "When you have that baby, I am leaving you!" I felt like someone had sucked the air out of my lungs. What was going on with this man why was he saying these things to me, especially now?

I looked at him angrily and said, "What do you mean, 'that baby'? This is our baby, not a 'that.' What is wrong with you?

Maybe all the rumors are true. More than one person has told me that you have been seeing someone!"

Billy denied he was seeing anyone. He said he was tired of being married, and he wanted to go back to Denver with his family. Billy had found new friends that were selling cocaine, and he was planning on going to Denver to hook up with some dealers. He said he could make good money quickly. I couldn't believe this man. Now he was tired of being married, involved with drugs, and the new friends he was hanging out with were drug dealers. I didn't believe anything he was saying to me. He was changing back into the person he used to be.

Before my eyes, Billy was slowly changing again; he would push me away and was irritable. He was never affectionate or loving. Our marriage was going downhill fast, and I didn't know what made him change. Now he was saying he didn't want to be married anymore and that he was leaving and hearing "I don't love you anymore," crushed me to my core. What had I done to make this man that I loved and had been married to for years would look me in the eye and say, "I don't love you anymore?" I began having panic attacks when I would think about him leaving me with two children. I couldn't afford to pay a new mortgage with my part-time job. It was too much pressure on me.

I never shared what I was going through with anyone; only God knew. I would talk to him and share my heart and pray that this situation would change. I put on a happy face and would pretend everything was good in our lives and that we were so in love with each other.

The stress that Billy put me through caused me to go into labor three weeks early. My water broke, and we headed to the hospital. I was in labor for two days before they decided to perform a c-section. I thought I was going to die. They gave me a spinal epidural to help with contractions and numb the pain. Hospital staff told me I would not feel a thing. That was not the case. I felt everything. The pain I was in was the worst pain physical pain I had been through in my life!

I delivered a baby boy. I named him David. He was so small he weighed five pounds and ten ounces. Chuckie was so excited to have a baby brother he loved him as soon as he laid eyes on him.

Billy drove home with Chuckie that night; the hospital was thirty miles away. My dad was worried about me and didn't leave my side that night.

Billy would come to visit in the evenings for a half-hour, then he would leave. He still had it in his head to move back to Denver. I couldn't see losing everything to go back to Nothing. He didn't have a job or a home in Denver.

The day I went home from the hospital, Billy announced, "I decided to stay here in Alamosa with you and the boys." I was happy he wasn't leaving me with two boys after I had just got home from the hospital, but I still didn't trust him. I knew he was up to something.

Billy's actions did not improve. He didn't take care of the boys and me. I was so thankful my mom would come and help me in the mornings with the boys until I started feeling better.

Billy's attitude didn't change. He was still cold and distant. It was so hard to be in a loveless marriage. The depression completely made me lose my appetite. I couldn't eat when I was around Billy. He was so rude and mean to me, everything I did would irritate him. I felt like I had to walk on eggshells when I was around him. I didn't want to fight with him, especially in front of the boys, so I would take his rude comments and swallow my tears. I was happy when he was away at work, and I didn't have to deal with him.

When David was three months old, I went back to work part-time at the pharmacy. I had only been back to work for three months when Billy had a change of heart and decided he wanted to move to Denver as a family.

I couldn't understand why he wanted to move back to Denver. We had a nice home, and he had a good job. He didn't have a home for us there or a job. I didn't know what he was thinking. He said, "I need a change. I am tired of living in this small town. There is so much more for us in a bigger town like Denver."

I prayed and prayed for direction from the Lord. I didn't have a great feeling about this decision Billy had made for us. His selfishness shined through, and I knew he hadn't considered us at all. He quit his job and took Chuckie with him to Denver, the city where he grew up. He was going to find a job then come back for David and me.

He left me with the task of packing up the house. I worked at the pharmacy during the day and packed every evening. I missed Chuckie so much. A week without him seemed like an eternity. He was my buddy, and he helped me so much with his brother, but most of all, I missed his hugs and kisses.

After two weeks, Billy came back to Alamosa with Chuckie. I heard the car pull up, and Chuckie ran in the door and called, "Mom, I'm home. I missed you so much!" I hugged and kissed him until he said, "Enough, Mom, you gave me too many kisses!" That boy was my joy, and my heart overflowed with love for him.

Billy was cold, as usual, and said he had found a job at a low-income apartment complex, and they would be giving us a free apartment. I was so sad. I was going to miss my family. It was going to be so hard to be away from them.

My mom cried. She was going to miss us so much. "You know we're always here if you need us for anything." My parents had always loved and supported me.

We left the next day to start over again. I prayed for strength and wisdom! I knew this wasn't going to be easy. I was going to the place filled with bad memories, and I hated it. But I didn't want my boys to grow up without a father, so for their sake, I did whatever it took. I would stay with their father to keep this

family together

Time Moves On

We moved into one of the apartments and started our life again. I missed my beautiful home and my family. I met some of the women who lived in our building and started building friendships.

Billy began to change so much he had met a few guys who sold drugs and thought he could make extra money for us. I was so against this I was scared for my sons and me. One evening when the boys were in bed, Billy pulled out a package and told me he was holding it for one of his friends. He was looking for a place to hide it. I was so angry with him. I told him, "If the police come to our apartment and find those drugs here, they will take the kids from us! Please get it out of here!"

Billy became angry. "Nothing is going to happen! I am just going to hold it overnight!" I made him take the package of cocaine out of the apartment first thing in the morning. Nothing was more important than keeping my boys safe. Billy wanted to make extra money for us and had taken up with drug dealers. I told him, "You took us away from the home I loved and my family so you could get involved with selling drugs? Living in an apartment in Denver and not having you around is not the life I want for our boys and me! It's not fair to have us in this situation with you." He laughed. "You worry too much. Nothing is going to happen. I am just going to make extra money. Everyone does it around here."

Billy started playing softball again. When he wasn't at the ballpark, he was with his new friends making money, which I never saw. He started neglecting the boys and me again. He was never around. I returned to the life I had seven years before, lonely and depressed. I couldn't understand what had changed Billy so much. He wasn't the same person anymore. All the memories flooded back. How did I get to this place again? We were happy for so long, and now my world was slowly falling apart. It felt like a slap in the face. I knew a storm was coming. I didn't know if I would have the strength to endure it, or would it crush me completely?

Chapter 5

The Storm

One beautiful Saturday morning, a few months after moving to Denver, Billy planned to take our two sons and me to pick up lunch and have a picnic at the park after he finished some errands. The boys and I got ready and waited for Billy to return. Chuckie was so excited and couldn't wait for his dad to get back. Chuckie had his baseball glove and ball ready to go. He picked out some toys for his baby brother. I was looking forward to some quality family time.

We were on our way to pick up some food when Billy turns to me and says, "I've decided to move out. I am moving in with my friend Al. I'm not happy with you, and I don't love you anymore."

I was furious! I told him, "You move me out here, away from my family again, and all of a sudden, you're not happy, and you've decided to move out and leave the boys and me again?"

I wanted to punch him in the nose. I began to shake. I couldn't believe he decided to tell me this in front of Chuckie. What kind of father doesn't care what he says in front of his kids? I started to cry. "I don't understand why you would say this, especially now, with our kids in the car." I looked at my seven-year-old in the back seat, and he looked as if his dad had just crushed his spirit.

Billy said, "I just need to get it out, and I figured now was a good time. We're going to get something to eat, and then I'll take you back home and get my things." Tears began to fall and run down my face as they had before, but this time, I couldn't stop them. I could barely breathe. My chest hurt each time I took a breath. My heart was beyond shattered, and the hurt in my son's eyes tore me in a million pieces.

Chuckie was excited all morning, and now he had just heard his dad say he was moving out! I continued to wonder what kind of man would blurt out these things in front of his children. I wanted to scratch his eyes out, but I couldn't move. Time seemed to be going in slow motion around me. I was frozen.

Billy looked at me and said, "I'm sorry things turned out this way, but I have to live my life and be happy, and you don't make me happy!" I was speechless. All of the hurt feelings from before came rushing back to me.

Billy realized he left his wallet at home, so we drove back to get it. He parked across the street and ran upstairs to the apartment.

I was in shock and couldn't move. I was crying. I should have hopped out of the car and taken the boys with me on foot, but I couldn't think straight. I felt my world crashing down. Everything around me started to fade, and I felt like I was going to pass out.

Chuckie unbuckled his seat belt and came to the front seat. "Don't cry, Mama." He began to wipe the tears from my face. He was sad, but he was trying to comfort me. I told him, "Chuckie, I'm ok, baby. Please go back and put your seat belt on."

Chuckie had just climbed back to his seat when I abruptly flew into the dashboard and hit my face. I screamed and flew back into my seat. Again, I flew forward and hit the window this time, hitting the side of my face. I looked up and saw a white car coming toward the front of my car again.

A young man had sped into the parking lot; he was driving drunk. He lost control of his car and hit my parked car head-on. He backed up and put his car in drive and proceeded to hit my car two more times. I was hurt. There was blood everywhere. I quickly looked in the back seat to check on the boys. They were both crying. Thankfully, they were safe. Chuckie would be bruised up, but there was no blood. David was in his car seat, scared.

Chuckie screamed, "Mama, you're bleeding!" He was crying. I told him, "I'm ok. I hit my nose and its bleeding. Don't cry. I'm alright".

Billy heard the sound of a crash. The impact of cars colliding was very loud. Billy ran out of the apartment; he pulled the guy out of his car and proceeded to punch him several times. The police and ambulance came. I was taken to the hospital. My nose was broken in two places, had two black eyes, and had bruises everywhere.

When I was released, Billy picked us up some food and took us back to the apartment. He said he was sorry for what had happened but was going to pack a bag and leave. He would be back for more of his things during the week. He hugged the boys and left.

I sat on the couch, holding my boys thinking about what had just happened. My world, as I knew it had just crumbled. Chuckie hugged me tight and told me he loved me. He was so worried about me; he kept asking me, "Mommy, do you need me to get you anything?" I assured him I was fine, and I just wanted to hold him and his brother. I just needed some hugs and kisses.

We lived in a low-income apartment where Billy worked as a maintenance man in exchange for an apartment. What was I going to do now? I was a stay at home, mom. I didn't have a job. I had just paid off my car, but now it was totaled.

I put my boys to bed and sat down in the corner of my living room and began to sob. "Jesus, I need you. I can't do this without you! I can't believe the events of this day. I am broken inside and out."

I wondered what I did that would make Billy would say, "I don't love you anymore," after all these years? There had to be someone else in his life. I had lived this before! My life was being ripped apart at the seams, shredded into nothingness. I was afraid to face life alone. The man I loved had abandoned his sons and me.

My chest felt so heavy, and it was hard to breathe, tears streamed from my eyes until I couldn't cry anymore. I went to the bathroom to wash my face, and once again, I didn't recognize the person in the mirror. I had two black eyes, a broken nose, and scratches on my face. I didn't look beautiful but ugly. I looked like a poor lost lifeless soul who reeked of failure, pain, worthlessness, and devastation.

Who could I talk to about what I was going through? Who would understand this kind of pain I was feeling? No one could! Every part of me hurt, I felt throbbing, stabbing pain over my whole body. I wanted to die or go to sleep and wake up and find it was only a nightmare. But this was a reality I knew all too well, and I knew Billy would never come back to us.

I was a good wife. I did all the things a wife should do to keep his home and his children clean, made sure there was food on the when he got home, supported him, and loved him, but it still wasn't good enough. How would I go on alone? How can I raise my beautiful boys alone? I was so afraid of the future, but I had two little boys that I loved. They were my world, and with the help of God, would make it.

I cried myself to sleep that night. I didn't see Billy until Monday morning. He came back to the apartment to change into his work uniform. He looked at me and said coldly, "How are you feeling? You look terrible." I told him I was in pain, but I would heal.

He hugged the boys and turned to me. "Here are the keys to my car. You can use it if you need to go anywhere today." I thanked him, but I knew there was nowhere I needed to go. I didn't want to see anyone with two black eyes and a swollen nose. I didn't see Billy for the rest of the week. Friday came, and I knew it was payday. I was running out of food. I knew Billy would be coming around to get his car. I waited for him.

I saw him and frowned. I asked, "Why haven't you come by to check on the boys? They are missing you." He looked at me and shrugged his shoulders. "I have been busy and haven't had a chance to get back to the apartment." I didn't want to fight. I told him, "We need food and other things. Aren't you going to give me any money? I know you got paid today."

He looked at me angrily and pulled out a hundred-dollar bill and threw it at my feet. "Go get on welfare. That is where you belong." He laughed at me and walked away.

I hated Billy. He was so full of himself and didn't even care about his kids. I knew he was seeing another woman. He always acted this way when there was someone else. The words I heard coming out of his mouth stung. "You belong on welfare." I never wanted to depend on this man again. I had to come up with a plan to get us out of this messy situation.

My car was demolished and undrivable. I got my boys up on Saturday and put my little one in his stroller, and we walked to get a few groceries. I tried to make it an adventure for Chuckie since we never had to walk anywhere. He was sad. He asked me, "Did I do something wrong? Is that why my dad left me? Are we still buddies forever? Dad always said we would always be buddies, but we don't see him anymore?"

My heart broke for him. He loved his dad so much and looked up to him. I tried to encourage him. "Dad will never stop loving you, and you'll always be his best buddy. I know he will come and see you soon."

On the way home, we took a different street. Billy's car was parked on the side of the road. Chuckie said, "Look, Mom, there's Dad's car. Why is it parked here?" I told him I didn't know. I looked inside, and there was a pair of red high heels and a red belt. I thought, "What kind of woman dates a married man with children?" I wanted to see her and ask her this question.

I was so angry I wanted to pull her hair out and throw a few punches, but then I decided she could have him. Billy wasn't a good husband or father. He was very selfish and only cared about himself. I should have left the first time that little high school girl came to my door, but I gave him another chance.

I didn't want my boys to grow up in a broken home, no matter what he did, I always forgave him. I wouldn't ever take this path again. The pain was too much to handle. I was done with him. During our seven years of marriage, there had been so much betrayal and heartache. Now abandonment was the final factor. My emotions were all over the place. I cried when I was alone. I didn't want my boys to see.

I was determined to go to college and make something of myself. I got a part-time job and applied for school grants. I did apply for assistance to help with some of the finances. I never again would I let a man make me feel like I was a nobody and not good enough. I enrolled in Denver Community College.

Billy never gave me any money apart from the hundred dollars he threw at my feet. He rarely picked up the boys. He would call and say he would pick up the boys on Saturday. The boys would wait all day, looking out the window, but he never came or called to say he was sorry he couldn't make it. He not only broke my heart, but he also broke the heart of his sons.

Chuckie always looked so sad. Every day he would ask, "Do you think my dad will come and see us today?"

I was so angry with him. After this behavior happened a couple of times, I wouldn't let him see the boys. I told him, "They wait all day, staring out the window, and you never come. You hurt them, and it's not fair to them that you never come."

Billy was seeing another woman. I found out her name was Susan and her mother lived on the other side of the apartment complex where we lived. Billy had moved in with her not long after he left us and rarely came to see the boys. When he did, it was only for a few minutes. He would say, "I can only stay a moment. Susan doesn't want me in your apartment." I would reply, "I don't care what Susan wants; you to have two small boys who miss their dad!"

It was hurtful to see Billy driving by after work with Susan and her son in her nice car. I let the boys go with him a few times, but Billy was never in their life. I filed for a divorce, and I swore to myself I would never let a man step all over me again. I hated Billy

for abandoning his family for another woman.

Chapter 6

Giving Love A Second Chance

After the devastation I had endured with Billy, it took a few years before I thought about dating again. How could I trust a man with my heart again? I didn't believe there were any good guys.

Then, I met Joe. I enjoyed his company. He was fun to be around. I was lonely, and it was nice to have someone trying to capture my heart. He would bring me flowers and take me to nice dinners. He made me feel beautiful and special. Joe started attending church with me, and he was good to my boys, and they liked him.

We dated for a year then he asked me to marry him. I was so happy to be in love again and ready to begin a new life with this wonderful man. Little did I know a monster lived in him. Joe had a terrible temper and was a very jealous man.

The first time I experienced his abuse was a few months after we were married. I was working at one of the hospitals in town, and Joe came to see me. I was talking with one of the male nurses when he walked in. He initially had a smile on his face and asked if I could take a quick break. He needed to speak with me outside.

We walked outside, and he suddenly took the key to his car and stabbed me in the stomach with it. He was angry. "Who was that guy, and why were you flirting with him?" "I wasn't flirting with him; we were talking about a patient." I was shocked, and I said to him," What is wrong with you? You hurt me!" He was furious. "You better come straight home!"

I was so angry with him, but I didn't want to cause a scene. I walked back in, and my friend asked me if I was ok. She had seen him shove his key into my stomach. I told her I was fine. She asked me, "Does he hit you?" I told her, "No, this is the first time he has ever acted this way. I don't know what is going on with him."

She asked, "Will you be all right going home with the way he is acting?" I assured her I would be fine.

My stomach hurt where he stabbed me with the key, but thankfully it didn't pierce my skin, but I had a deep scratch on my stomach. I couldn't understand why Joe had been so angry and violent. He had always been so loving towards me. I got home and went into the house, but the boys weren't there. They were hanging out with their friends.

I was so angry at Joe. I sat down and asked him, "What was that all about, you coming to my job and hurting me? Just because I was talking to another man, you got violent with me. What is going on with you?" He said, "I was watching you for a while, and you were laughing and flirting with him. I will not put up with that!" I stood up. "I am not going to argue with you, and I will not put up with you abusing me!" I walked into the bathroom to change. I wasn't aware that Joe followed me until he grabbed me by my hair and threw me to the floor. I hit my face so hard, and my nose began to bleed. Everything went black for a few minutes. I slowly got up off the floor. Joe had left the house. I started to cry as I got in the shower. I thought about what kind of a man I had married. I had never seen this side of him, and it scared me.

I had waited so long to find love again, and now I was married to a man that hit me. I had never experienced this before, and it was scary to be in a relationship like this. I was afraid he was going to get aggressive with the boys. I didn't want them to know what had happened.

Joe came back home. He said he was sorry, and he would never do that again. He still scared me. I didn't know when he was going to flip out and if he would hurt me again.

One evening when he picked me up at the hospital again, I was talking to the nurses, and he saw me. I saw that look on his face, and I said to myself, "Not again. He is already mad." I said hello to him and tried to make conversation. He just looked at me with a disgusted look on his face.

I took a deep breath, got in the car, and waited for the explosion to begin. I was so scared I was shaking inside. He began to drive out of town. I knew there was a lake out there. I prayed we weren't going there. I couldn't bear the thought of not seeing my kids again. I asked where we were going. He spat at me and grabbed my hair and shook my head around. He spoke with such an angry voice, "I saw you talking and laughing with those men! Who knows what else you do all day!"

He wouldn't let go of my hair. I began to scream. I begged him to let me go and take me home. I explained, "Those are the people I work with! I have to communicate with them! What is wrong with you? Please let go of my hair and take me home. You said you would never hit me again!" He laughed. "I'm not hitting you; I'm pulling your hair! That's different!" He let go of my hair. Tears were streaming down my cheeks. I wanted to get far away from him. I hated him. He tormented me all the way home, grabbing my hair and yanking it from side to side.

I was hoping David would be playing with the neighbors' kids. I knew Chuck wouldn't be home. Chuck spent most of his time hanging out with his friends. He didn't like being around Joe. His attitude toward the boys changed when we got married.

When we got home, I got out of the car and ran straight to the bathroom and locked the door. I looked in the mirror, and my face was swollen from crying. I brushed my hair out, and chunks fell out. I was so devastated. How was I going to get out of this marriage?

Who Was I Married Too?

My first marriage had been so devastating, but it was nothing compared to this new marriage. I thought I was going to be so happy when Joe and I got married. It turned out there was a monster living inside of him.

Every time Joe hurt me, he would say, "I am so sorry. It will never happen again. I know I have a bad temper, and I let it get the best of me!" I wanted to leave, but I didn't know what he would do to me or if he would try to hurt the boys, so I stayed and prayed for a way out.

I didn't tell anyone what was going on. I felt so ashamed for the circumstance I was in and thought to myself, "Another failed marriage. I hoped things would be different this time and that I had found someone who loved me and would treat me special."

The abuse continued. It was not only physical but verbal and mental. He wouldn't let anyone see this side of him. Only me. To others, he was the perfect, loving husband. He everyone fooled.

He went to the gym every evening. I would see him giving himself shots, and I saw his mood change even more. Now he was angry all the time. I had to walk on eggshells when he was around. I didn't want to live like this and have my boys in this environment.

I got so annoyed at myself for putting up with the abuse. I needed to make a change. I just wasn't ready to share with anyone what I was enduring. I didn't want my friends or family to suspect what was going on. I needed help. I didn't know what to do.

The next time he hit me, I grabbed two brass candlesticks. I shouted, "I am tired of you hitting me whenever you feel like it! What kind of man are you? Come near me again, try to put your hands on me again, and I will take these candlesticks and kill you! You will never touch me again! I hate you!"

Joe's mouth fell open, and he said, "Ok, I will leave you alone. I won't hit you again. I'm sorry, really sorry, for the way I have treated you, please forgive me!"

I didn't believe him, but I meant business. I didn't care what I had to do; I would never let him touch me again. Enough was enough! I understand how women who are abused just snap one day and end up killing their husbands. I would have done it in a heartbeat and wouldn't have cared. I got to a point where I was going to defend myself with whatever I could get my hands-on.

I didn't trust him, and I wasn't going to forgive him for the things he said and did to me. When he would say, "I love you," those words that would make my heart sing didn't mean anything to me now. I had lost all respect for this man. I didn't love him, and I wanted out of this marriage. I had to get out. I knew it was going to take a little time, but I would get out!

Secrets

After that day, things were never the same between us. Joe tried to make things better between us, but I didn't want it anymore. I hated it when he touched me, and he made my skin crawl. He was going to church every Sunday with me, but I carried bitterness and hatred for him.

I struggled with my faith. I couldn't forgive Joe for what he had done to me, and I knew he would hit me again if I weren't on guard. I never told anyone about the abuse I had endured. I kept it held within my heart. I put on a happy face wherever I went, and we acted as the perfect couple when we were around friends and family.

One day, I got home a little early and needed to get a few groceries. Joe had forgotten to leave me money. I jumped in my car and went to the gym where he worked out. As I approached the doors, I saw Joe standing off to the side off to one side on the phone. I quietly walked up to him, but he didn't hear me. He was laughing and talking sweetly to someone. He turned around and hung up real fast. "What are you doing here?" "You forgot to leave me money, and I need to go to the grocery store. Who were you talking to?" He played it off and told me he was talking to one of his friends that were supposed to meet him at the gym but were running late. I knew he was lying. I took the money and left. Now, I knew he was cheating on me. I guess I didn't blame him; we didn't have a marriage anymore.

When Joe got home, he was waiting for a fight, but I didn't say anything. If I had mentioned the phone call, I knew he would deny any accusations. If he got angry, he would try to hit me again, and I would fight back. I knew the time would come when I would be free.

Joe began to stay later at the gym or go out after work on Friday, with his buddies for a drink. He would come home late and make excuses. I knew he was with a woman, but I didn't care. I was happier when he was gone. I didn't have to always be on guard when he wasn't home.

One morning, Joe jumped in the shower, and I was gathering up the dirty clothes to start laundry. When I picked up Joe's pants, his wallet fell out. I picked up the wallet, and a receipt from Macy's fell out. I glanced at the receipt as I was putting back in the wallet. It was for perfume. Before I could stop myself, I confronted him. He looked at me and told me he bought the perfume for a friend.

My jealousy flared. "You buy perfume for a friend? What about me? You never buy me perfume!" Joe yelled, "Put my wallet away! You don't deserve anything from me!" He took a swing at me but missed as I backed away from him. He then grabbed the bottle of shampoo and threw it at me. I backed away and threw his wallet and the receipt on the floor and slammed the bathroom door shut.

I put my shoes on as quickly as I could, found my car keys, and left. I didn't trust him. He was angry. I knew he would be leaving to work shortly, and then I could go home. I had caught him, and he was furious. What friend had he bought expensive perfume for? I knew he was seeing another woman. I didn't understand why he just wouldn't let me go. I despised him. His temper was out of control. I didn't know what to do.

Later that evening, he called to say he was sorry for hitting me with the shampoo bottle. He told me it was my fault for snooping in his things. He told me if he wanted to buy things for his friends, I shouldn't tell him anything. It was his money, and he could spend it on what he chose. He then asked, "Are you sorry for starting this fight and making me hit you?" I knew if I didn't say, "Yes, I'm sorry. I won't touch your things again," he would come home and fight with me. I gave in and told him what he wanted to hear.

Searching for The Truth

My friend Rachel called me a few days later and mentioned she had seen Joe at the mall. He was sitting talking to one of the girls that worked at the bank in the mall. "They looked pretty friendly. He was so into her; he didn't see me. I'm sorry if I hurt you by sharing this with you, but I felt you needed to know."

Her name was Jessica. My sister went to school with her. I knew her very well; she was always cheating on her husband.

Rachel kept saying she was sorry to bring me bad news, but she couldn't let the situation blindside her friend.

Even though I didn't love Joe, it still hurt my heart to know he was cheating on me and had found someone else to spend his time with. How was I going to confront him? I knew Joe would go into a violent rage if I didn't have ammunition to confront him. How was I going to get the proof I needed to confront him and end this marriage for good?

I called my brother and asked him if there was a way to record conversations on my home phone. I shared what my friend Rachel had told me. My brother felt so bad for me. He told me what to buy, and I set up my home phone to record every conversation. I was going to have the proof to confront him and tell him I was going to divorce him.

I knew Joe wouldn't divorce me. He wanted to control me. I prayed I would get the ammunition to get the divorce. Joe would not want his family to know that he was cheating. He wanted to keep pretending we were happy.

He was working the night shift so he would be home sleeping during the day. I prayed that I would find something on the recorder when he left for work. I couldn't wait for Joe to leave that evening so I could check the recorder. To my surprise, there were no calls made out.

I knew in my gut he was cheating on me with this girl, and I needed to find the proof. I contemplated going to the bank and confronting her myself, but as I thought it through, this was a bad idea. Jessica could deny it and tell Joe. The fear of his violence put a fear in me.

Each day Joe would come home from work in such a bad mood and complain about everything. He tried to hit me a few times, but I always grabbed something to protect myself. I would tell him, "You better sleep with one eye open. If you touch me, you may never make it out of that bed."

He would laugh at me and say, "I was just messing with you, I wasn't going to hit you. I promised you I wouldn't." I knew I had to be on guard. I didn't trust him.

Every day I would check the recorder and find nothing. I was ready to give up when, bingo! Joe had called the bank and asked to speak to Jessica. He asked her if could take her to lunch. He told her he had missed talking but had been busy at work and hadn't had the time to stop by the bank.

He sounded annoyed when she turned his invitation down. He asked her if they could meet up for a drink on Friday. She said she wasn't sure and would call him back. That was the end of the call.

The call did reveal Joe was trying to get this girl to meet him, but I didn't have enough to confront him. I knew I had to continue to monitor the calls until I had enough information to prove he was cheating.

In the next couple of weeks, he made several calls to her and would ask when he could see her again. She would always say she would call him later.

I began to pray, "Lord, show me the things that have been hidden in darkness. Bring them to the light." I was so miserable, I just wanted out of this marriage, but I knew Joe would not let me go that easy.

I had told Joe many times I wanted out of the marriage, that I wasn't happy. He would always say, "You can't leave me. I won't let you leave me! I won't have my friends and family think I was a bad husband. If you leave, I know you'll open your big mouth and tell everyone I was mean and abusive, which is not true. It's all in your head! I refuse to have people lose respect for me because of you."

Finding Freedom

I had saved money to rent an apartment for the boys and me; they had already been through enough with Joe. This marriage was over. I was getting ready to leave the house and look at an apartment. Joe parked his car directly behind mine, and I didn't want to wake him up, so I took his keys from his pants and proceeded to move his car. It was then that I found all the proof I needed to get away from him. There was a letter on the passenger seat addressed to Jessica. I opened it up and read it. In the letter, Joe confessed his love for her, and there were details of their times together. The letter was what I needed and prayed for. I took the letter and put it in my trunk. I was going to take it to Joe's sister and share everything I had endured. I was going to divorce him and be free once and for all.

I was going to take control of my life. I found an apartment and could move in within days of signing the lease. I wasn't afraid anymore. I pulled up to the house a few hours later, Joe came storming out of the house and hit the hood of my car. He was beyond furious. He yelled at me, "Get out of the car and give me back the letter!" He began to swear and tried to open my car door. I backed the car up and took off down the road. There was no way I was giving him the letter. It was proof of his deceit.

I looked in the rear-view mirror, and he was chasing me in his car. I was so scared. What I was going to do? I had to think of a place where he could not get his hands on me. I saw a bar up ahead and parked my car. I ran in there as fast as I could. I prayed someone would help me if he came in chasing me. Just as I reached for the door, Joe pulled up in his car, screaming, "Come here! I won't hurt you! I just want my letter!"

I sat down at the bar and looked around. It was busy in there. I saw two big guys and asked them for help. I told them my husband was after me and was going to hit me. I was terrified of him. They turned out to be good guys. They told me they wouldn't let him come near me if he came through the door.

Joe never came in, and I finally decided to leave. These two kind young men walked me to my car and asked if they could follow me home to make sure I got back safe. I agreed. I was so nervous and scared. I didn't see Joe's car, and then suddenly he was behind me. He drove his car up beside mine and tried to run me off the road.

The two guys that were following me were behind Joe and were witnessing what was happening. They began to honk and put their high beams on Joe's vehicle. Joe realized the men were following him. He turned down another road. Joe was gone. I was praying that I wouldn't see him again that night.

I got home safely; the two kind young men followed me. They gave me their phone numbers and told me, "If your husband comes back, call the police and let them know you have two witnesses who saw him try to run you off the road." I thanked them and called them my guardian angels, who helped save me.

Joe never came home that night. I was so thankful. I didn't sleep, I was looking out the window waiting for the headlights as he pulled into the driveway, but they never came. I had the phone in my hand, ready to call the police. There was no way I was going to let him in.

The next day while I was at work, Joe came home and got his things and left. I made a copy of the letter and took the original letter to Joe's sister and shared everything that had happened. She felt so bad that I had been too scared to confide in anyone. She said she was going to speak to him.

I told her I just wanted a divorce, and I for him to leave me completely alone, and if he attempted to contact me, I would press charges. I knew he would probably lose his job if word got out that he had abused his wife and tried to run her off the road. I told her about my witnesses, and I stated they would testify if I pressed charges.

When I got home that evening, there was a message on the answering machine from Joe. He was full of remorse for what he had done and stated he was going to get the divorce and was so sorry for all he had put me through. I moved out that weekend, and in a couple of weeks, following, I received divorce papers.

I could finally breathe again. The nightmare was over. I never wanted another man in my life after the cheating and abuse I had endured. How was I ever going to trust and love again?

Chapter 7

Look at My Canvas Now

My once beautiful canvas is now torn, dirty, and stained. Did the Father still see me as a Masterpiece? Where is the beauty it once possessed? I could only see the tear stains, the bloodstains from the deep wounds, and the rips in this canvas that once was beautiful.

How would God put me back together again? I was broken, and my heart wounded from unmet expectations and betrayal, both men who said they would love, honor, and cherish me for the rest of my life.

One man abandoned my children and me to live a life with someone else. He verbally abused me to the point that I hated who I saw in the mirror. Although I was no longer a chubby girl, I had lost all the extra weight, but each time I looked at myself in the mirror, I saw an overweight person.

When I was married to Billy, he put the thought in my head that I was overweight, and after he left me for someone else, I started to believe he left because of my weight.

The abandonment led me to have no self-confidence. I did not want to eat, except to function. I became anorexic and depressed, and I could not eat properly. My stomach was always in knots. I couldn't get better because I would continue to think of him with his new family when he had two beautiful children.

My children suffered just as much as I. I remember Billy coming over to see the boys one Sunday after church, and Chuckie looked at him with such sad eyes and said, "Daddy, I am so sorry that I was a bad boy. Please, forgive me, and come back home!" I felt sorrow. I saw the pain in his eyes. He was so desperate to have his dad back. He thought it was his fault his dad had left. I looked away as the tears began to flow down my face. I couldn't help but cry. My little boy would do or say anything to get his dad to come back home.

I was so angry. Billy was a selfish man and didn't see what he was doing to our son. Chuckie's heart was broken. I wanted to punch him in the face and beat him senseless. In my mind, I was beating him and screaming, "See what you have done to your son!" I felt so helpless looking into my child's eyes, knowing his life had crumbled just as mine had, and it would never be the same.

My baby was just as broken as I was, how could I fix him when I couldn't even fix myself! The only thing I could do was to love him with all that was within me and try to provide a better life for him.

Years later, out of loneliness, I took a chance to love again, but this time it almost cost me my life. Joe said he loved me but had not shown any love for me. The physical abuse proved he didn't love me. Joe took me through a journey of what I thought was love, to feeling defeated and worthless. I thought the second time in a marriage would be different. In reality, this relationship was so much worse than the first.

I was so disappointed, frustrated, and ashamed of two failed marriages. Only God knew my secrets and the depth of my pain.

I was lost. I was buried somewhere along the way, beneath the rubble of brokenness, still alive, but barely breathing.

I was suffocating and slowly dying. Only God could dig me out and make me whole again.

I'm Drowning!

Isaiah 43:2 - New Living Translation (NLT)
"When you go through deep waters, I will be with you"

Have you ever felt like you're drowning and can barely keep afloat? That is exactly how I felt. My heart was beyond shattered at this point in my life, and it was a heap of dust.

The memory of the hurt and pain that I felt when Billy left flooded my thoughts and my heart again. The abuse and pain I had gone through with Joe just about took me over the edge.

I cried out to God, "Save me from this death! I want to live again! Please help me find myself. I know she is here somewhere; I just don't know where to find her!"

When I walked out the door each morning, I felt like a put a mask with a smile on it. I was hiding my pain. I was slowly dying inside and didn't know how I was going to get through the day.

I would pray and cry out, "God, please help me, please heal my brokenness! I want to live again. I feel like I am dying. Your word says you heal the shattered heart, and please heal my shattered heart!"

I knew I had to someone I could talk to and share what I was going through. I couldn't carry this alone. It was time to trust someone who could guide me. I went to church on Wednesday and asked the pastor's wife Amanda if I could meet with her for some counseling. She was more than happy to meet with me. We scheduled an appointment for the next evening.

I was so nervous about meeting with Amanda, but I knew I needed help. I was always a private person, only letting people see who I wanted them to see, and it was usually a happy person. I never wanted to show the real me that carried so much hurt and pain. We prayed together, and then I began to share my heart with her. I began to speak, and everything I had been holding in began to pour out like a river. I cried as I revealed everything I buried.

Pastor Amanda prayed for me and told me I had to stop holding everything in. She would be there for me to help me heal.

I knew God would always be with me and help me to heal. His word says, "When you go through deep waters, I will be with you!" I had been in very deep waters for years. I desperately need to be rescued. I needed a Savior! I was going to do everything I could to get free and find the person I lost.

Heal My Broken Heart

Psalms 147:3 - The Passion Translation (TPT)
"He heals the wounds of every shattered heart."

When you're suffering from a broken heart, it can be very difficult to quiet your mind and shut it down to get some rest. Sadness, grief, and depression can overwhelm a person and take you to a place where you would rather sleep than face the world! Depression is a horrible place to be. It's like falling into a very deep dark hole, and you've lost all the fight that is in you just to climb out.

I carried deep wounds from the hurt I endured with Billy and Joe. My pain was constant and felt never ending.

I remember one evening after my boys had gone to bed, I put worship music on and began to sing to the Lord. The tears began to run down my face as I began to sing. I knew there was nothing that could heal my broken heart except God. He was the only one that could restore my brokenness.

It surrendered everything I was carrying, all the hurt and the pain. I got down on my knees and began to weep and said, "Jesus, you are the only one who knows how broken my heart is right now, and I need you to heal me! I'm tired of carrying all this pain that I've carried for so many years!"

I knew I had to forgive every person who had hurt me. I didn't want to hold on to bitterness anymore. It was slowly killing me, like cancer. I listed everyone out loud. "I forgive them all, Lord. I release this hurt and pain I have been carrying. Please heal me and make me whole again." I felt like a warm blanket had been placed on my shoulders; the pain in my heart was gone.

Peace came upon me. I couldn't stop the tears, and they just flowed and flowed. I couldn't stop thanking Jesus for taking the hurt and the pain away. I knew my life would never be the same again.

I had an encounter with the lover of my soul. He was pouring his love all over me, washing my heart of the hurt and pain I had been carrying. All I had to do was surrender and forgive, and the weight lifted off of my life. I felt free. A peaceful presence came over the room. I laid on the floor and cried until there were no more tears. I sat up and took a deep breath and thanked God for his love and mercy in my life.

The hardest thing in life is to let go and surrender everything to the Lord. Sometimes we just don't realize how much God loves us and wants to heal us and free us from emotional bondage.

I encourage anyone who is carrying hurt and pain to surrender to the lover of your soul. He will heal you and set you free. It doesn't take a fancy prayer.

The Father just wants to hear you give everything to him and ask for healing.

Prayer for a Restoration of the Heart

First, you must forgive the person or people that have hurt or offended you. Then, you need to ask for healing.

Father, I come to you and surrender everything I have been carrying. Father, I forgive _____ for hurting me. I ask forgiveness for the anger, bitterness, and unforgiveness in my heart against _____. I receive your forgiveness. Please heal my broken heart and remove the pain that I have been carrying. Give me peace and joy again, restore my heart. In Jesus' name, I pray, Amen.

Chapter 8

Walls Around My Heart

Ezekiel 36:26 - Amplified Bible (AMP)
*"Moreover, I will give you a new heart and put a new spirit within you,
and I will remove the heart of stone from your flesh and give you a heart
of flesh."*

Many years had passed since the deep pain in my heart
was healed. I had now built emotional walls around my heart. The
mental and physical abuse had caused trauma.

I was afraid to fall in love again; I had experienced so much
heartache with the two men that I had loved that I never wanted to
endure pain again. I dated now, and nothing ever lasted. I found
myself attracted to men with the same characteristics as the two
men I had loved. I guess I always went back to the familiar. The
fear of being betrayed and deceived made it hard to trust anyone.

How many of you reading this book have ever felt this way?
Have you also built walls around your heart because of the pain

you experienced? Let me tell you what walls do to your life. Walls around your heart make you feel protected from the pain, but the problem with walls is that love and kindness can't get near you. When you live in constant fear of being hurt by the next person that wants to love you, you keep them at arm's length and eventually push them away.

I had placed walls around my heart like a fortress. I failed to recognize these walls were also limiting what God had called me to do, and everything God had intended for me.

In 2004 I was ordained as a minister, and through the years, I have worn many hats. A pastor, a worship leader, a teacher, and a mentor. I had a heart for the broken and wounded, and my greatest desire was to see them healed and free from pain. It was easy for me to love others, but I didn't know how to receive and accept love. Fear always held me back.

I always felt disconnected. I wanted to have close friends, but something was always in the way. I kept people at arm's length, thinking, "I can't let you get too close to me. You might hurt me". Few people knew the real me because this thought was always running through my mind.

I could be in a room full of people and feel like I was on the outside looking in. Fear of being hurt had me bound for many years. How could I mentor and pray for freedom for everyone else but keep myself from getting emotionally healed?

You can hide your feelings from everyone, but you can't hide from God. God began to deal with me about these walls that I had placed around my heart. One Sunday after church service. One of the ladies that I knew came up to me. "You have walls up, and you only let a minimal amount of people into your circle. Unless you bring the walls down, you will never get to the destiny God has for you." I was in shock! She must have read my face because she told me, "I am just obedient to give you the message that God gave me for you."

Talk about a slap in the face! This was a wakeup call for me. I thanked her and let her know she was right. I did have walls up, and I knew they needed to come down. The walls I had put up were in place for protection, but I knew it was time to deal with the issue of fear and distrust. I had to trust God and bring down the walls that had encircled my heart.

I had been hurt deeply, and it was easy to put walls up as protection, but self-protection is not the same as God's protection. Self-protection keeps the emphasis on self, and self-protection had kept me from trusting the people which God placed around me.

The word of God says he is my defender, my protector, my vindicator, and my healer. I had to trust that when the walls came down, the Lord would guard my heart.

I had to be willing to open my heart and take a chance. No one ever wants to experience emotional or mental pain. I knew it was time to take the walls down. I came to the realization, if I kept these walls up, my life would never be healed, and the enemy would win. I could see the enemy laughing at me, and it made me furious to think I had believed a lie all these years. It was time to heal completely.

I knew I could never go into a new relationship with the baggage from the past. I had to get these walls that I had built removed to trust and love again!

It was time to surrender and bring the walls down brick by brick. These walls were hindering God's plan for my life. Behind these walls, no one could hurt me, but I couldn't do what God had called me to do. If I had the walls up, God couldn't touch others through me. More than anything, I wanted to help others to achieve their healings.

It was time for the warrior that was deep inside me to rise and change the situation. I knew who God created me to be and he wanted me to live a life full of love.

I got down on my knees and surrendered everything that I had held on to. I visualized the walls around my heart, and I took them down brick by brick. This was not as easy as it sounds; each brick had been placed there to protect me. I began to weep and pray as I pulled each brick down from the wall until there was nothing left around my heart. "Father, in the name of Jesus, tear down the walls around my heart that have kept me emotionally trapped. Remove the barriers of hurt, fear, panic, and anger that have separated me from your abundant life.

I felt a release; a blanket of love surrounded me. I cried, but this time the tears were there because of the immense joy I was feeling. I wanted to be filled with love, and I prayed the following prayer. "Father, in the name of Jesus, I receive restoration to my mind and my emotions. Fill my heart layer upon layer with your love in Jesus' name Amen."

The walls surrounding my heart were gone entirely. I felt so free. I began to laugh. It surprised me because this laugh was different; it was the laugh I had as a young girl. It is truly amazing how God can restore even the sound of laughter.

For the first time in so many years, it was wonderful not to feel like I was on the outside looking in. I was more confident and open to new friendships and perhaps finding love again.

Since that day, I have been hurt many times, but the difference now is I forgive, and I don't hold on to words or actions. I remind myself not to build walls again. Nothing is worth stealing my joy and taking me back to that lonely place. I don't want a wall ever to encircle my life. I've learned how to be free and trust my defender, my protector, my God!

As you read this chapter, I pray those who have walls around your heart decide to bring the walls down and live again. I know some of you are saying, "That's all? A simple prayer?" It takes a willingness to bring your walls down and a simple prayer. God is looking for a willing heart. He wants to bring freedom to your life today.

Are you ready to knock down those walls that have kept you bound? God has a plan for your life. Don't let fear hold you back from the future that has been written about you! Below are the prayers I prayed to bring down my walls. My prayer for you is to be free and live life filled with joy.

"Father, in the name of Jesus, tear down the walls around my heart that have kept me emotionally trapped. Remove the barriers of hurt, fear, panic, and anger that have separated me from your abundant life."

"Father, in the name of Jesus, I receive restoration to my mind and my emotions. Fill my heart, layer upon layer, with your love. In Jesus' name, Amen."

Chapter 9

Wounds in My Soul

3 John 1:2 – New King James Version (KJV)
"Beloved, I pray that you may prosper in all things and be in health, just as your soul prospers."

The Father loves his children so much he wants us to live a life filled with love. You see, He is love. Again, He reminds me that he doesn't see me the way I do. He sees me as his perfect beautiful masterpiece.

Can you remember the last time you felt whole and complete? There was a time when I couldn't. There were deep wounds in my heart, and these wounds needed complete healing. Today, my walls have come down, and I am not afraid to let people in and around my life, and I am ready to love again. God loves us so much he wants us to have complete restoration. I wanted to be restored and live life the way God intended, to be free and prosperous, but I knew there was much more that needed to heal.

I began to pray and seek God for answers on soul wounds. God began to take me on a journey of healing my soul. Every trauma I had been through, every word that had been spoken against me or over me, from the time I was a child until a few years ago, had caused deep wounds in my soul.

Have you ever heard a song and the memories come flooding back, and you relive the hurt and the pain over again? The anger rises in you as the memories come rushing back and you tell yourself, "if I ever see him or her, "I'm going to give him or her a piece of my mind for all the things they ever did to me!"

Wait! I was healed of all that pain, what is going on here? Although you may have prayed for healing of your heart, there is still cellular memory, and soul wounds are connected.

Each of the chapters of my life with Billy and with Joe created deep wounds. A young girl of nineteen so naive marries the love of her life, and she is wounded by the young man she thought she would grow old with. But you see, she didn't know he had wounds that he also carried. Billy didn't know how to be a husband or a father because of the example he had growing up.

I found love again, but Joe had anger issues. He would hit me because of his insecurities. When I wasn't enough, he turned to other women for comfort. He was just as broken as I was. Two broken people cannot fix each other. It was a recipe for disaster.

I wanted someone to love me to give me the affection I so desperately thought I needed. I desired a man that would put me first in his life and treat me like I was special. Joe did make me feel loved, and he did treat me special until I had a ring on my finger then the real person emerged this relationship added even more deep wounds to my soul.

Psalm 147:3
"no heart is too shattered; no wound is too deep. He heals the wounds of every shattered heart."

God wants to heal each of us completely of every wound that is in our heart so we can move on to our future. When we surrender everything, Jesus takes all the shattered pieces of your heart and gives a new heart. God wants you to be whole, and he takes the brokenness of our lives puts us back together even better than what we were before.

It's essential to understand what it means to have a wounded soul and how it can affect, control, and devastate every area of your life. When your soul is wounded, you often wound other people. The condition of our soul is not only felt by us, but it is also felt by those we are in a relationship with. Sometimes unintentionally, many times we don't even know what we are doing.

Your soul is operating all the time. It is impacted by everything you speak, everything you watch, everything you read. You're constantly feeding your soul life or death. .

What is A Soul?

Genesis 2:7 - King James Version (KJV)
"And the Lord God formed man of the dust of the ground and breathed into his nostrils the breath of life, and man became a living soul."

As we read the scripture above, God did not make a body and put a soul into it like a letter into an envelope. But he formed man's body from the dust, and then, by breathing divine breath into it, he made the body of dust live. The dust did not embody a soul, but it became a living soul whole and complete.

God created us as a three-part being with a body, soul, and spirit. The soul is our will, emotions, mind, intellect, and imagination the inner part of you. The bible, which is the word of God, clearly states that God created each one of us this way.

1Thessalonians 5:23 – New International Version (NIV)
"May God himself, the God of peace, sanctify you through and through. May your whole spirit, soul, and body be kept blameless at the coming of your Lord Jesus Christ"

The soul is composed of three elements: a mind to think, a heart to feel, and a will to decide.

What is a soul wound?

When you accept Jesus as your savior, your spirit is made whole, but it's the soul that goes through a process to be made whole.

When the soul is wounded, it is called an inner wound. A soul wound is inflicted on the soul through the gateway of the mind, will, emotions, feelings, and trauma.

A soul wound is an emotional hurt that has not been addressed. Not only does your past affect your present and your future, but everything you have held onto creates wounds in your soul. When the soul is wounded, we hurt other people with our words and our actions.

When there is an inner wound that has smoldered, it becomes easy to lash out or have sudden outbursts of anger, hate, resentment, etc. You may find it easy to lash out at people who love you and have done you no harm. Just like physical wounds, if not treated, can cause death to our bodies, inner wounds do more damage because these are wounds, we can't see.

I also caused wounds in my soul with the things I had placed in my soul, such as unforgiveness, anger, and bitterness. I prayed and forgave those who had hurt me deeply. I had to search my heart, and I asked God to forgive my sins and forgive me for wounding others with my actions and my words.

The health of your soul can affect and control every part of your life. A wounded soul impacts everything, every single part of your life. It changes your will, cause you to make wrong decisions, and to think wrong thoughts. Soul wounds also cause you to feel painful, negative, and hurtful emotions.

These wounds impact every area of your life. They are often responsible for adultery, divorce, and business failures. A

Ihaven't.

soul wound can affect your health and can cause cancer, viral infections, and other debilitating diseases.

In the forty-three years that I had been serving the Lord and going to church I had never been taught about healing of the soul or the inner places of the heart. I began to educate myself and find anything that pertained to the soul. I had to understand how to heal my soul, how to free myself from the pain that still lingered.

Soul Wounds

Life presents endless challenges, trials, pressure, and sometimes persecution. No one is exempt from them. Burdens in the soul can be so significant they drive people to give up and lose all hope.

That is how much power soul wounds have on a person. I know from the experience of feeling so much loss and

I Am A Masterpiece

abandonment, I wanted to give up. I found myself spiraling into depression, and I didn't know how to overcome it.

Soul wounds have the power to devastate us and wipe out every ounce of hope and sometimes life itself. Have you ever felt so hopeless because of the hurt in your heart, and you didn't know if you go on with life? Wounds affect your mental state and can take you to a place where you contemplate hurting yourself or even at times ending your life.

According to the word of God, our souls are wounded through two primary sources sin and trauma. The Prophet Isaiah writes in chapter thirty the day that the Lord binds up the hurt of His people and heals their wound [Inflicted by Him because of their sins].

Sin can wound you, and even though you have accepted Jesus Christ as your Lord and Savior and his blood has cleansed you of all unrighteousness and brought you into a right relationship with God, there are still wounds in your soul that need to be healed. Sin can also wound your mind. Once your soul has been injured and wounded by sin, it needs healing.

Psalm 41:4 - King James Version (KJV)
"I said, Lord, be merciful unto me: heal my soul; for I have sinned against thee."

Sin and trauma damage your soul and affect so many areas of our lives. There are times we don't even know wounds exist; they are buried so deep. Ninety percent of sickness is caused by emotional distress.

Wounds created from sins against you

Any sin can leave a wound or a scar in your soul. Your soul can be wounded when other people sin against you; they talk behind your back or accuse you of something you didn't do when people have abused you verbally, physically, and sexually. Your soul is also wounded when you are abandoned, rejected, and neglected. Pain and fear can make you feel so helpless.

When you hold on to these wounds, they can cause sickness. I suffered for over twenty years of migraines and bleeding ulcers because of the wounds I carried. When I got healed of the wounds in my soul, and I was restored, my body healed completely.

Wounds created by our own sin

Romans 6:23 - New International Version
"For the wages of sin is death, but the gift of God is eternal life in Christ Jesus, our Lord."

We commit sins by gossiping, lying, being dishonest, stealing, fornication, committing adultery, alcohol, drug use, just to name a few. We medicate ourselves to numb the pain. The gravity of the sin doesn't matter, in terms of the harm it can do to you. Sin can wound every part of you, including your mind.

When you whisper words of gossip or speak evil against someone, it can create deadly wounds in your soul.

Proverbs 26:22-Amplified Bible, Classic Edition (AMPC)

"The words of a whisperer or slanderer are like dainty morsels or words of sport [to some, but to others are like deadly wounds, and they go down into the innermost parts of the body [or of the victim's nature."

According to this verse, words create deadly wounds in a person's innermost parts of the body. When you gossip and speak evil against someone, it can create such hurt and pain in his soul that those wounds become a threat to that person's life. Those words of gossip and evil cause deadly wounds to form in your soul.

Proverbs 14:3 - Amplified Bible, Classic Edition (AMPC)
"A calm and undisturbed mind and heart are the life and health of the body, but envy, jealousy, and wrath are like rottenness of the bones."

Jealousy and envy will wound your soul and cause your bones to become brittle and rot.

Proverbs 17:20 - New International Version (NIV)
One whose heart is corrupt does not prosper; one whose tongue is perverse falls into trouble.

This verse tells us gossip and slander also affect your finances. Do you wonder why you are always having problems with your finances or other areas in your life? It could be because of the words you have spoken about others.

Trauma

The condition of your soul can directly affect the health of your physical body. The first sign of trauma is a sense of shattering or being torn apart from the inside out.

Trauma is a common cause of illness. It has the power to open doors of our bodies to sickness, and it gets our bodies out of alignment and can experience extreme weight loss, insomnia, nervousness, and anxiety.

A disturbing experience causes trauma, for example, a tragic accident, a death in your family, a chronic illness, being abandoned by a parent or by a husband, the loss of a job, financial setback, or mental, physical, or sexual abuse.

The effects of trauma can cause intense emotional fluctuations, unhappiness, anxiety, loneliness, anger, and irritability. Have you ever felt like you are on an emotional roller coaster due to some sort of trauma? One minute you are okay, then something triggers the memory you have been through, and suddenly your crying uncontrollably, or you get so angry you want to hurt someone or even hurt yourself.

The trauma of betrayal, abonnement, or divorce produces a unique, emotional, violent blow to the body, heart, and mind. When this type of trauma happens, we feel like we can no longer deal with reality, the pain is too great and signals the brain that our life is under threat.

When I read the word of God I am taken to the story of Job, he went through horrible tragedies losing his children, grandchildren he lost everything in one day. Job mentions the word soul 23 times he says my soul is being poured out, he is vexed in his soul, mourning in his soul. Job expressed the excruciating pain he felt in his soul.

How many of us can relate to Job? I know I can, because of the several tragedies I have endured in my life.

Soul wounds control your emotions

Psalm 88:3 - King James Version (KJV)
"'For my soul is full of troubles: and my life draweth nigh unto the grave."

Do you ever feel fearful, anxious, angry, or depressed? Are you always worried or annoyed, or do you complain and argue with everyone? During conflicts, do you scream violently or cry uncontrollably?

If you answered yes to any of these, your soul is deeply wounded. I know because I was guilty of all these. Many years I dealt with these emotions until my soul was healed, today I am a new person, and I have peace in my soul.

Soul Wounds Cause Physical Sickness

The condition of your soul can directly affect the health of your physical body. Offense is one of the primary sins that wound people and makes them sick. Sickness can be caused by offense and make you physically ill because you sin and are holding on to offenses. Unforgiveness eats away at your body and emotions releasing stress hormones that weaken your immune system

We are all wounded to some extent. When your soul is wounded, various kinds of trouble can come into your life.

Psalm 103:1-3 - King James Version (KJV)
"Bless the Lord, O my soul: and all that is within me, bless his holy name. Bless the Lord, O my soul, and forget not all his benefits: Who forgiveth all thine iniquities; who healeth all thy diseases"

Soul Wounds Cause Demonic Assaults

Ephesians 6:12 - King James Version (KJV)
"For we wrestle not against flesh and blood, but principalities, against powers, against the rulers of the darkness of this world, against spiritual wickedness in high places."

According to this verse, the spirits we wrestle with are rulers over the darkness. The darkness in your soul, the hate and unforgiveness you carry, are open doors for demonic assaults. This darkness in your soul is what gives evil powers the right to rule over your life.

Wounds in your soul can not only make you physically sick; they can also give demonic spirits the right to attack every part of your life, including your physical body. Soul wounds cause long-term disorders and prevent healing.

I had a very wounded soul until the day I decided to get free and restored of all the wounds from trauma, the wounds from sin, and the wounds upon me, which were caused by others. My prayer is that each person who has finished reading this chapter will have a desire to receive your healing and live a life of abundance.

Chapter 10

Healing your Soul

Psalms 23:3 - King James Version (KJV)
" He restoreth my soul: he leadeth me in the paths of righteousness for his name's sake."

In the book of Psalms, Chapter 23, it states that God restores my soul. He wants to heal us everywhere; we hurt just as our body needs healing. Our souls are sick and need to be healed. The soul is the inner part of us. If your soul is wounded and bleeding, you will never enjoy life. You will feel disconnected like something is missing or like you are always on the outside looking in.

It's time to confront, perhaps re-open these wounds and expose the infection, and be rid of the poison so that they can heal properly. The journey of healing your soul will take time. It's peeling away at the layers and removing the Band-Aids that you placed on your wounds. It's time to lighten the load and stop carrying baggage with you; the suitcases are filled with the pain from your past. They are heavy and burdensome.

It's time to be the person God intended you to be after all, we are created in his image. The enemy wants to keep you in your past, never to move on to what God has promised you.

Jesus didn't offer his life just so you could be saved and spend eternity with Him in heaven, but also so you could be healed and live on earth in true peace, joy, and happiness. Jesus came that we may have *and* enjoy life, and have it in abundance *"to the full, till it overflows." (John 10:10)*

You can choose to go on trying to get through each day and admit that you have had enough unhappiness, hurt, shame, and misery in your life. You must decide for yourself, and as an act of will, choose today to take control of your life. Are you ready to do whatever it takes to be whole and at peace?

This journey of healing my soul helped me to understand how these wounds came to be.

Every trauma I had been through, every word that had been spoken against me or over me, from the time I was a child until a few years ago, had caused deep wounds in my soul.

The memory of the pain I had endured was still buried deep within my heart, my soul, and I was still a wounded vessel. Not only does your past affect you in life, but everything you have held onto creates wounds in your soul.

As I was writing this book, I began to weep as I remembered the pain of rejection and abandonment. Although I found healing so many years ago, the cellular memory was still there. I had to also pray for the cellular memory to be removed.

I began to pray and asked the Holy Spirit to show me the wounds that I still carried. The memories came flooding into my mind. I had childhood memories of being bullied, and teachers that were not so kind to me.

I forgave every person that had hurt me with their spoken words. I asked Jesus to heal the soul wounds that had been caused by these hurtful words.

I asked Jesus to put his blood that he shed for me on these wounds and make me whole. I did this daily for six months as the Holy Spirit would remind me of a situation that had caused a wound. There were times I would weep uncontrollably with the memory, and no matter how much it hurt, I faced the pain and forgave and asked Jesus to heal that soul wound.

The Holy Spirit would reveal to me if I didn't forgive a person. I would search my heart and forgive them and ask Jesus to heal the soul wound. To this day, I ask the Holy Spirit to search my heart and reveal to me if I have a soul wound.

Once the wounds were all healed, it was as though I was reborn again. I have such joy that I never knew could exist. I can honestly say this is how it feels to be free the chains have indeed fallen, and I can rejoice in a new life. I may carry scars on my body of the trauma of my past, but when I look at these scars, they now have new meaning. I have overcome, and God has healed me.

I found myself again when I was completely healed. Although It took many years, I love the new and improved me.

Psalm 31:8 - The Passion Translation (TPT)
"You have kept me from being conquered by my enemy.
you broke open the way to bring me to freedom,[a]
into a beautiful, broad place."

You see, I am no longer a victim of my past, but I am victorious in my present. I am a Masterpiece one of a kind made by the Creator himself fashioned so uniquely that no one has my smile or my laugh. I can look in the mirror and see a beautiful, loving, strong woman. I love who I have become because of letting go and letting God heal me.

Although I have been a Minister for many years, I can genuinely say I have a more significant, deeper walk with the

Lord. My greatest desire is to help others with their journey to being healed body and soul completely.

The enemy tells us we are not good enough because of our past mistakes because he knows if we discover the truth, we become unstoppable.

Chapter 11

Prayers to Set You Free

Today, I walk in freedom, and I no longer carry wounds in my heart. Today, I live life with joy. I laugh and love like never before. I walk in freedom, and the chains have truly fallen. I rejoice in this new life I am now living.

I am no longer a victim, but I have risen from the ashes with beauty and strength. Let go of the past and present pain and allow God to heal the deep wounds in your heart and embrace you with his perfect love.

The Father created each one of his children uniquely, and you are of a kind, created with perfection, and you are his treasure.

Today, I invite you to ask Jesus Christ to be the Lord of your life.

Dear Lord Jesus, I know that I am a sinner, and I ask for Your forgiveness. I believe You died for my sins and rose from the dead. I turn from my sins and invite You to come into my heart and life. I want to trust and follow You as my Lord and Savior.

Next, forgive. Jesus forgave your sins now; you must forgive those who hurt you. Ask the Holy Spirit to reveal the wounds that you are carrying, and one by one, pull the bandages off and pray the prayers below to heal the wounds in your soul. Remember, this is a process; it is a journey of healing.

Jesus died on the cross to save us, to heal us by his blood; we are healed body and soul. The Dunamis power that raised Jesus from the dead that power will make you whole.

Lord Jesus, I ask that you heal every wound in my soul. I believe you can wash my soul clean of every sin that wounded me and every sin I placed in my soul. Heal me of every trauma I have lived through and remove all cellular memory associated with the trauma—Wipeout all my generational sins and wounds in my bloodlines. I believe you are the lover of my soul and will heal every wound in my soul with your Dunamis power in Jesus' name. Amen.

~

Father as an act of my will, I chose to lose all darkness, all hate, all confusion, all grief, all misunderstanding, all fear, all offense, any unforgiveness, any torment, any addiction whether to a person, place or thing. Any witchcraft anything of the enemy right now I lose it from my soul in Jesus name. Amen.

~

Father, as an act of my will so my soul will prosper. I choose for you to download into my soul with your love, your life, your joy, your presence, your plans, your revelation in Jesus' name, I receive it. Amen.

~

Father, I repent for all my sins, known and unknown. I repent and ask for forgiveness that my soul might be cleansed.

Father, I repent for speaking against another person. I am so sorry every unkind word that came out of my mouth, please forgive me, and heal these wounds in my soul. I plead the blood of Jesus over my soul and ask you, Jesus, to send your Dunamis power your Dunamis light to heal this area of my soul. Amen.

My Prayer for you is to be genuinely free and understand who you are in this life. You are a beautiful masterpiece painted with love.

Printed in Great Britain
by Amazon